THE YOUTH WORKER'S BIG BOOK OF CASE STUDIES
NOT QUITE A MILLION STORIES THAT BEG DISCUSSION

The Youth Worker's Big Book of Case Studies: Not Quite a Million Stories That Beg Discussion
Copyright © 2003 by Youth Specialties

Youth Specialties Books, 300 South Pierce Street, El Cajon, CA 92020, are published by Zondervan,
5300 Patterson Aveune SE, Grand Rapids, MI 49530

Library of Congress Cataloging-in-Publication Data

Case, Steven L., 1964–
  The youth worker's big book of case studies : not quite a million
stories that beg discussion / by Steven L. Case.
      p. cm.
  ISBN-10: 0-310-25562-7 (pbk.)
  ISBN-13: 978-0-310-25562-8 (pbk.)
  1. Church group work with youth—Case studies. I. Title.
  BV4447.C3785 2004
  259'.23--dc22

                                                                    2003015185

Editorial and art direction by Rick Marschall
Edited by Jim Kochenburger
Proofreading by Anita Palmer
Cover design by ArtParts
Interior design by Rayburn Design
Design assistance by Sarah Jongsma
Editorial Assistance by Ted Marschall
Printed in the United States of America

07 08 09 10 • 10 9 8 7 6

BIG BOOK

THE YOUTH WORKER'S BIG BOOK OF CASE STUDIES

NOT QUITE A MILLION STORIES THAT BEG DISCUSSION

ZONDERVAN®

GRAND RAPIDS, MICHIGAN 49530

ZONDERVAN.COM/
AUTHORTRACKER

Youth Specialties

www.youthspecialties.com

INTRODUCTION

Craig Wilson, the noted speaker and performer, once said, "You shouldn't have smoke coming out of the windows in the youth room…you should have FLAMES."

That's what this book is intended to incite.

The Youth Worker's Big Book of Case Studies is not an easy book to use. It will not give you warm and fuzzy feelings about Jesus. It will not take difficult situations and wrap them up in pretty packages with happy-ever-after endings.

This book *will* give you a place to start those wonderfully loud discussions that will make the walls of the youth room vibrate. Herein you will find difficult situations that will make your students glad they are not the ones in the stories—although they very well could be. Some of the stories are fairly light in tone; others will make your teens (and maybe you, too) uncomfortable.

This book will not give you any easy answers. In fact it will give you a lot of difficult questions.

It also provides you with scripture references that might have the effect of throwing gasoline on the fire instead of making kids feel better. There are no answers, let alone easy ones, to some of the things that life throws at us.

Most of these studies do not have conclusions. The conclusion must take place in the youth room and in the hearts and minds of the kids in the days that follow the sessions flowing from this book.

Here are some things we've designed in the book to make it user-friendly: The Case Studies are categorized, so you can present what you want—or need—to your kids. But they are arranged at random, just like life. Therefore we have more than the usual Table of Contents: 1) a normal list of Case Studies as they appear in the book. 2) a Table of Categories, so you can reference the major themes, which are also ID'd on each page. 3) a Table of Topics, in which we highlight the variant themes or subplots, so you can be more creative in picking, choosing, and combining lessons; these are ID'd on the edge of every page, like a file folder.

Then on appropriate pages, we have provided areas where you can "take notes and make notes." When reading a Case Study, you might be reminded of something personal to you that can enrich the story when you share it; or some comments that might warn students of content or make a point more meaningful; or you might want to construct a variation. Make notes. Also, on the Questions side of the Case Studies, note taking/making areas invite you to add your own challenges and applications for students, add Bible verses that speak to you in a different way, or prompt you to direct discussions in a certain direction. This book should be a workbook of kids-under-construction, not a collection of mere stories, lists, and scripts.

Our job as youth workers is not always to find the answers but to ask the questions that need asking and let the discussion go where it goes. Let's trust the Holy Spirit to do the rest.

Being a Christian is hard. Jesus did not promise to solve all our problems for us. He did, however, promise to be there, beside us, through everything. The stories here deal with topics like integrity, honesty, faith, love, family, and all the rest of the things that drive us crazy. And they are presented primarily to get your students to do something we almost never ask them to do in the church…THINK.

THE INCREDIBLE SHRINKING YOUTH GROUP

Dan belongs to the youth group at a church that hired a new youth minister a year ago this week. Under the previous youth minister, youth meetings were always a fun place to go on Sundays. Every week 50 to 60 teenagers showed up. In addition, they had a youth group calendar packed with cool activities, like concerts, ski trips and amusement park trips.

Over the past year, under the new youth minister, attendance has dropped from a weekly average of 50 teenagers to just 15. The group has gotten a lot more serious. Instead of fun ski weekends, the group goes and works at homeless shelters and participates in work-camps-helping fix up homes for poor people. The new youth minister has serious discussions and asks hard questions about life and the future-stuff that Dan doesn't want to think about.

A bunch of Dan's friends who no longer come have invited him to a church a few miles away that's like how their youth group used to be. It seems "everybody" is going there. Dan has to decide which group he would like to belong to.

DISCUSS:

- What's the big deal?

- Does it matter which youth group Dan attends? Why?

- Aren't the fun and fellowship in the other group important as well as the serious stuff in Dan's youth group? Why?

- Should a youth group be more fun or more serious? Why? (What are the positive reasons for having a fun youth group? Negatives? What are the positive reasons for having a serious youth group? Negatives?)

- What are the most important things Dan should consider as he decides between youth groups?

- What's the difference between learning and being taught?

- What's important in this situation?

Read:

Matthew 13:9; Romans 8:28

- Think back over your life from a year or so ago to now. When have you grown the most as a person? Explain.

- How does your experience apply to Dan's decision?

- If you were Dan, what would you do?

TEACHER'S PET

David has Mr. Hawthorne as his teacher for two classes. Nobody likes Mr. Hawthorne. He gives a tremendous amount of homework and doesn't seem to care about his student's personal schedules and he doesn't put up with any fooling around. He has assigned more detentions and called more parent conferences than any other teacher. For some reason, Mr. Hawthorne likes David. He respects his work and says David shows "promise."

Spring Break is coming up and Mr. Hawthorne traditionally assigns a huge term paper to be turned in the day school resumes. Several of David's friends have asked him to use his influence with Mr. Hawthorne to talk him out of the assignment in order to protect their cool Spring Break plans.

David doesn't want to fall from Mr. Hawthorne's good graces, but he does want to have a good time on Spring Break with his friends.

    © **Is this teacher's expectation reasonable? Why?**

    © **How easy is it to tell your friends "No"?**

© **How much respect do your teachers get from the students in your classes? How much do they get from you?**

© **Is respect earned or is it given to everyone, until you have reason to do otherwise?**

© **Who was the best teacher you ever had? Not your favorite but the one who was best at their job?**

© **Should the students just stop moaning, suck it up and do the assignment? At what point? Why?**

© **How difficult a situation is David in? Explain.**

Matthew 5:14-16
1 Timothy 4:14

© **What role does "pleasure-seeking" play in David's difficult situation? Explain.**

© **If you were David, what would you do to be respectful to Mr. Hawthorne? How would you respond to your friends?**

11

OBEY THE RULES OF YOUTH MINISTRY

Becca is a talented artist. When her friend Nicole was injured and had surgery on her knee, Becca visited her in the hospital and painted a Hawaiian beach scene on Nicole's cast. The woman who shared the room asked Becca if she would paint a design on her cast as well.

Before she knew it, Becca had done more than 20 paintings on various patients' casts in the hospital. She made friends with the nurses and the patients loved her artwork.

Several doctors complained that patients were not resting and staying in their rooms—they had taken to wandering around showing off their cast artwork.

One doctor told a nurse to ask Becca not to paint casts anymore since it was interfering in her patient's care (and the patients of other doctors). Becca has been considering this a mission or a ministry of her own.

She is heartbroken over not being allowed to paint casts anymore.

DISCUSS:

@ **What is the most important part of recovering from an operation or broken bone?**

@ **What is most important to the "healing" process?**

@ **Why would the doctors want their patients in their rooms?**

@ **When you come up against rules that keep you from doing something you want to do, how should you respond? Why? What about when rules keep you from doing something you feel God wants you to do, how should you respond?**

@ **Is it important for Becca to try and understand the doctor's rules? Why?**

@ **Should Becca obey the doctor's rules? Why?**

@ Define "mission."

@ What is the best way to react when a kindness you want to show is rejected/ stopped by another person? Explain.

@ Are most rules put in place for a reason? Can you think of an example?

@ What happened to some of God's best messengers?

Read: Psalm 103:1 Luke 19:40

@ How does this passage apply to Becca's situation?

@ How can Becca best let her light shine...by painting people's casts or by obeying the doctor's rules? Why?

@ Would you go back to the hospital? Why?

TAKE NOTES/MAKE NOTES

MY BROTHER'S SHADOW

Rich is 16 years old. He had an older brother named Mike. When they were little, Mike was diagnosed with MS. Their mom soon spent all of her time taking care of Mike. As a result, Rich often felt lost in the shuffle when he was younger.

Most things the family did were for Mike. The family schedule revolved around Mike. Mike's surgery and treatments kept the family strapped for cash and they went without things other families had.

Mike died last year. The family was devastated by the loss. After awhile Rich hoped he could build a close relationship with his mother, only to find that even Mike's memory caused her to shut him out completely.

She always talked about Mike and shared favorite memories. She barely acknowledged Rich's achievements and good qualities.

When Rich brought home his first-ever report card with all "A"s and "B"s his mom only said "I remember when Mike got straight "A"s. Rich talked to his dad but he dad only said the "Mom will come around—give her time."

Rich doesn't know how to talk to his mom, but every day his hurt grows deeper. He struggles with jealousy and guilt over it because of his brother's death.

He wants to talk to his mother, but does not want to upset her.

TAKE NOTES/MAKE NOTES

DISCUSS:

@ Do we ever have a right to be jealous?

@ Is Rich's father wrong? How so?

@ Have you ever known someone who wears depression like a blanket? What happened?

@ How can "sorrow" be addictive?

@ What are the issues Rich is trying to work through in regard to his brother? His mother?

@ If you were his friend and he shared all this with you, what would you say or do? Why?

@ Is Rich right to feel a little jealous? Hurt? Left out? Why?

@ If you were Rich, how would you have responded to Rich's dad when he told Rich to give his mom "time"? Why?

@ After a year, do you think she should be over the loss of her son? Why?

Read: **John 16:33**
Psalm 19:40

@ How can Christ help Rich overcome the issues he is facing? The feelings he has?

@ What would you do if you were in Rich's place?

SIBLING RIVALRY, PARENTS, DEATH

SHOULD I STAY OR SHOULD I GO?

Tom's dad has a drinking problem. He has been in and out of AA (Alcoholic's Anonymous) several times but has never completed the program. When he drinks he abuses Tom and his mother—not physically, but with mean, cutting words.

He has been in and out of jobs and many bills are going unpaid. Collection agencies call regularly. Tom's dad was recently "written up" at work for coming back from his lunch hour drunk.

Tom's mom tells him she just can't take it anymore. She intends to leave Tom's dad to go live with her sister in another state. Tom is almost 18 and will graduate next year.

He doesn't want to leave his friends he has gone to school with since kindergarten, but the thought of living alone with his father is really depressing.

She has told him that she would like him to come with her but will understand if he stays behind.

TAKE NOTES/MAKE NOTES

DISCUSS:

What do you know about alcoholism? Do you know an alcoholic? Explain.

What does it mean to "cut your losses"?

What's the rule about the oxygen mask on a plane? How does that apply here? Should it?

How long should a person stay in an abusive situation?

Is it possible to love an alcoholic parent? Explain

If Tom came to you angry or depressed about his dad's drunken ranting and raving, what would you say? What would you do? Why?

Tom's mom has decided to leave his father. Is that the answer for Tom—leaving? Why?

How can Tom honor his mother in this situation? His father? Explain.

Does honor thy father and mother include the loss of your own life?

Read:

1 Timothy 4:12
Romans 8:38,39

In what way can Tom be an example for his parents and others in speech, life, love, faith and purity?

If you were Tom, what would you do?

FREE COOKIES-KINDNESS GONE BAD

Martha was shopping for a new pair of shoes at the mall on a Saturday morning. She found a 20-dollar bill folded up and lying on the floor.

Martha decided to have some fun. She bought a cookie at a place in the food court and told the cashier to keep the change—but to buy cookies for everyone who came up to the counter for as long as money lasted. Martha stood off to the side far enough away so that she could see people's reactions. She enjoyed herself so much that she went back the next weekend and spent her own money to do it again.

This time one of the customers was a reporter. The story of the "free cookies" made it to the paper. Shoppers mobbed the cookie place hoping for a freebie—but then they left without buying, so business slowed down. Others wrote to the paper to criticize the cookie place for staging a publicity stunt. Mall security received a series of complaints about a strange man offering children free cookies and then trying to lead them out of the mall—so parents became critical of the cookie giveaways as well.

Ultimately, the cookie place won't let Martha pay for free cookies anymore. Martha was surprised that her act of kindness was being seen as something bad. She is distraught. She wonders whether or not this will always happen when she tries to do nice things for others. This time one of the customers was a reporter. The story of the "free cookies" made it to the paper.

People began showing up to the mall hoping for a freebie. Others wrote in to the paper to criticize the "mysterious benefactor" as some sort of criminal who was teaching children that they should expect free things and take cookies from strangers.

Martha would like to let the whole thing drop but someone has now asked the police to check the mall security camera to find out if the person behind this is a wanted felon.

DISCUSS:

@ Have you ever heard the phrase "No good deed goes unpunished"? True or false? Explain.

@ Ever been treated ungratefully for doing something nice? Punished in return for something nice you did? Tell about it.

@ How can you keep being the "good guy" when it seems the world is waiting to bring you down?

@ If you were Martha...after this incident, would you have sworn off doing any more acts of kindness? How would you have responded? Why?

@ The world is a dangerous place. It's no wonder people don't trust each other. Should we stick with the people we know and not stick our necks out? Why?

@ What would you do if you were Martha? Explain.

Read:

Psalm 16:1-10
Proverbs 3:31
Hebrews 12:14-15

@ How have you been blessed by showing kindness to others in the past?

@ No matter what kindness we do...there will always be someone ready to criticize us or who will try to stop us. What can we do to not grow weary in doing good when this happens?

HOME SWEET HOME OR BATTLE ZONE?

Jack is 18 and a senior in high school. Jack's dad used to beat his mother occasionally. Some of Jack's earliest memories of his parents were of his father punching his mother. Jack's mother left them a year ago.

Jack has a 14-year old sister he has always looked out for. He has always tried to hide the "bad stuff" from her. Last week, Jack came home from football practice to find his father smacking his sister around. Jack lost it. He grabbed his dad and threw him against a wall.

The two fought hard, but Jack was stronger and eventually hit his father and knocked him out.

A neighbor called the police and both men were taken into custody. Jack's sister spent a few days at a friend's house. The police have asked Jack if he wants to file domestic violence charges against his father.

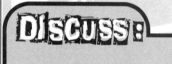

DISCUSS:

@ Why does it seem like God misses stuff sometimes? Explain.

@ What should Jack and his sister tell the police? Why?

@ How far should we take "honor thy father"? Should they forgive their dad...and just put this incident behind them? Explain.

@ What has fighting ever solved?

@ Where does hate come from?

@ If a friend of yours who lived in a violent home asked you, "Where is God when my parent beats me?" or, "If God is so powerful, why doesn't he stop the violence in my family?" what would you say? Why?

Read:

Exodus 20:11-13; Psalm 34:19 Mark 10:29; Ephesians 6:2

@ What might Jack and his sister pull from these passages to guide them in how to deal with this situation?

@ What would be your best option if you were Jack? Why?

THOU SHALT NOT BORROW

Rachel volunteers her time at a senior citizens' home. She began serving to get community service hours for school but has continued to go just because she enjoys it so much. She's become friends with a number of residents, but is particularly close to a woman named Agnes. Agnes was nearly 98 when Rachel first met her. They've spent lots of time together. Rachel reads the Bible to Agnes every time she visits.

Agnes has nearly died three times. All three times, her busy, businessman son rushes in to be there, but he doesn't show up at any other time. He's even complained to the nurses for getting him out of work for "no reason."

Agnes told Rachel that when her time comes, Rachel is to keep the Bible for herself. Rachel made a joke that she wanted Agnes to be there when she graduated from college and to not "make any other plans." Agnes just smiled and chuckled.

Agnes passed away in her sleep one night. Rachel found out the next day when she showed up to visit Agnes. Rachel went to Agnes' room and cried. A nurse came in and told Rachel that Agnes' son was on his way and that he had insisted, "nothing was to be touched" in his mother's room.

Rachel picked up the Bible Agnes wanted her to have. Then she remembered nothing was to be touched. The nurse smiled and said, "If I'm not here I didn't see anything." and walked out of the

Discuss:

@ What do you think of Rachel's work in the senior citizen's home? Would you serve in this way? Why?

@ Does the Bible belong to Rachel?

@ Why does it seem our culture ignores its elderly? Explain.

@ Should she just take the Bible and leave? Explain.

@ What if it wasn't a Bible but a priceless ring or bracelet? Explain.

Read:

Psalm 139:23-24
Job 12:12

@ If Rachel walked out with the Bible, would it offend God? Explain.

@ Pretend you're Rachel...what's your next move? Why?

IN THE DARK

Mike has been in an ongoing battle with his parents for a good six months—always over the rules.

He thinks he should stay up as late as he wants, hang out with whom he wants and go where he wants to go when he wants to go. His parents disagree to say the least. It has gotten to a point where they just try to avoid each other's company.

When he's home, Mike stays in his room, seeing no need to "talk to people who don't listen to me anyway." Mike's parents are tired of fighting with him and have let him withdraw from the family.

Mike is home alone tonight as a thunderstorm rages outside. His parents are gone for the weekend. Suddenly the power goes out in the house and Mike has absolutely no idea where to find candles, matches, or even a flashlight.

He is completely alone in the dark house. He sees only what is illuminated when the lightning flashes.

Sitting alone in his house, Mike begins to draw a comparison to his situation and his life. Due to the situation with his parents, he's spent the last several months sort of stumbling around in the dark, not knowing how to get himself out of the situation.

He knows he has to do something or he will be stumbling around in the dark for a long time.

DISCUSS:

@ **What are "growing pains"?**

@ **Why does it seem like we lock horns with parents every time we turn around?**

@ **How is your relationship with your parent(s) similar to Mike's? Different? Explain.**

@ **Why do you think Mike feels a similarity between his situation with his parents and stumbling around in the dark? Explain.**

How is parental guidance like light? Explain.

Will it ever be possible to be friends with your parents? Are your parents friends with their parents? How is it possible?

Think of one practical piece of advice you'd give Mike if you could call his cell phone right now, then "expand" that truth to a higher truth.

Read:

Deuteronomy 6:4-9
Psalm 139:23-24
Luke 5:16
1 Kings 3:12

In light of Mike's situation, and the passage you just read, what's Mike's best plan of action?

TAKE NOTES/MAKE NOTES

LEAVE IT TO BEAVER/COSBY

Kate has been pretty much living alone for the last four years. Her mother travels a lot for her work and Kate has become independent and self—sufficient. Her grades are good. She holds down a part-time job. She cooks, cleans and does her own laundry.

Kate's mom met a nice guy and started dating. Six months later they were married and Kate's mom decided to work from home. Kate's stepdad seems to want the whole Leave-It-To-Beaver/ Cosby home life-lots of family activities, family talks, and day trips. Kate feels smothered. She has made it on her own for at least four years. Having two parents who suddenly want to be a major part of her life is making her crazy.

@ **Your parents have seen you in diapers. Why might it be difficult for them to see you as an adult?**

@ **Would you say you are more or less independent than Kate? Self-sufficient? Why?**

@ **What happens when you do everything on your own?**

@ **Who has to do the adjusting in Kate's situation? Her or her parents? Why?**

@ **Is it a good thing or a bad thing that Kate's parents are now so available to her? Explain.**

@ **Who has to do the adjusting in Kate's situation—her or her parents? Why?**

@ **To hang out more with her parents, Kate will have to sacrifice some independence. If she does this, what will she gain?**

@ **Kate may lose some of the independence she has, but what will she gain?**

Proverbs 3:3-4
Matthew 7:24-27
Romans 8:24-27
Galations 5:2-5

@ **What would you do if you were Kate?**

SHOWER THE PEOPLE...WITH LOVE?

Doreen and Barb have been friends since kindergarten. They are both seniors this year. A little over a year ago Doreen began to date a boy that Barb didn't like. Neither did Doreen's parents. In fact, nobody liked him very much. Doreen is now pregnant and due in two months. Her boyfriend left town a few months ago and no one has seen him since.

Barb is invited to Doreen's baby shower. It will be a very small gathering, just family and a few friends. Barb's mother is opposed to her attending Doreen's shower. She will not forbid Barb from going, but she believes Doreen has committed a huge mistake and attending the shower supports her in her mistake.

- Did Doreen make a mistake? If so, should she be punished or banished or judged in some way? Why?

- If a couple has lived together for years and then eventually decides to get married...should they get a party? Why?

- Could you still be friends with someone who was convicted of murder?

- Could you still be friends with someone who went to jail for molesting a child? At what point would you say a person's behavior affects your friendship?

- Who gets to make judgments about such things?

- Do you agree with Barb's mother that Doreen has made a big mistake and should be shunned or avoided? Why?

- How might Barb and Doreen's relationship change over this?

- What does Doreen need most from Barb right now? Explain.

John 4:7-12
Psalm 139:23-24
John 8:7

- How would you advise Barb to show love to Doreen— while not doing anything that condones her mistake (makes Doreen's mistake seem okay)?

CLEANING JESUS

Ken just started a part-time, summer job as a custodian for his church. He will be assisting the current custodian on weekends and as a summer job. Ken's boss, Mr. Carter, is nearly 72.

Mr. Carter has a little trouble getting around but still manages to get the job done. Ken will be doing most of the heavy lifting while his boss handles most of the sweeping and dusting.

Mr. Carter has told Ken that there is something special about being a custodian at a church. He is fond of repeating "God is here and all the jobs we do should be done with the idea that God is watching." Ken looks at it as just a job.

Mr. Carter is extremely picky about the way Ken does things, right down to the way the statue of Jesus in the sanctuary should be cleaned. To Ken it's just a building to clean as quickly as possible and then go home. The carpet in the sanctuary is just a carpet not some sort of holy ground.

The longer Ken works there the more difficult the job seems to get. There seems to be no pleasing Mr. Carter. Ken can easily get a job flipping burgers and would never have to deal with his "crazy" boss anymore.

TAKE NOTES/MAKE NOTES

🌀 Tell of a time when you had to work for someone who thought nothing you did was ever good enough. How did you respond?

🌀 Should special attention be paid to "holy" places? Is the bathroom in a church holier than the bathroom in your school?

🌀 Define "Sacred."

🌀 Who is closer to being right: Ken who thinks cleaning the church is just a job? Or Mr. Carter who considers cleaning the church to be an honor? Explain.

🌀 As far as working at a job, is your philosophy closer to "good enough is good enough" or good enough is NEVER good enough"? Explain.

**Colossians 3:23
Hebrews 9:2
Ephesians 2:21
Matthew 18:20**

🌀 What are the differences in attitude between working for the Lord and working for men? Explain.

🌀 What advice would you give Ken about his job situation?

TAKE NOTES/MAKE NOTES

YOU SMELL SMOKE?

Chuck has bullied Matt since they were in kindergarten. Chuck has made it his mission in life to make Matt's life miserable. They are now in the 9th grade.

Chuck has been on a streak lately. No longer content with just making fun and the occasional punch in the hallway, he's begun shoving things into Matt's locker. Open ketchup packets, banana peels, and most recently a pack of lighted matches, which set off the smoke detector and cleared the school.

Pete, Matt's close friend, has often heard Matt talk about what he'd like to do to get even with Chuck. None of it has ever come to pass.

But lately Matt's plans to get even have become more elaborate and he talks about it all the time.

A few days ago Matt gave Pete a chilling look and told him he was "finally going to settle the score with Chuck" but would not say how. Pete does not believe that Matt will actually do anything.

But the tragedy at Columbine where two bullied kids went on a killing rampage are still fresh in everyone's mind.

DISCUSS:

❷ **Have you ever been bullied? What was it like?**

❷ **Are we overreacting to ideas of "revenge" because of the Columbine tragedy? Why?**

❷ **Why is sharing concerns about someone's plan to harm themselves or others criticized as "tattling" or "finking" bad thing? Explain.**

❷ **What can we do to remove the stigma that goes with "finking"?**

@ How do you imagine Matt feels, having been bullied by Chuck for 9 years?

@ Is Pete overreacting by thinking of Columbine and getting concerned for Matt? Explain.

@ Should Pete share his concerns about Matt with adults—or should he keep it all to himself? Why?

Read: 1 Thessalonians 5:13-15
Deuteronomy 9:2-3
Psalm 82
John 8:31-32

@ In light of this passage, how should Pete reach out to Matt?

@ Bottom line, what would you do if you were Pete? Why?

TAKE NOTES/MAKE NOTES

BROKEN MEMORIES

Scott and Brian have gone to their grandmother's house for a week during the summer since they were small children. They are now nearly finished with high school and they are back again.

Scott will be graduating and Brian has another year to go. They used to work with their grandfather on the farm until he passed away about four years ago.

Every time they visit, their grandmother gets out her memory box.

She removes all the contents and places them on the table. She lays out pictures and explains who each person in each picture is and how they are related. She pulls out a doll that she had when she was a child. A hair ribbon, a lock of hair, mementos, and much, much more. The box is crammed full.

Every year there is one item she pulls out of the box last, with much drama and fanfare. They know it is the snow globe that grandpa bought for her at the world's fair before he went off to the war. Scott and Brian have seen this all before.

Once again, she hands the snow globe to Brian who shakes it once and passes it on to his brother. Grandma is lost in the memory when Scott clumsily lets the globe slip from his hands and shatter on the floor.

TAKE NOTES/MAKE NOTES

@ What would your first words be, if you were Brian (other than THAT word)?

@ What would you do if you were Grandma?

@ How quickly would you forgive the person who broke or took from you a valued possession or memento? Why?

@ How could you make it up to someone that you had carelessly or accidentally hurt? Explain.

@ How quickly does forgiveness come? Does it depend on the crime? Why?

@ How might Scott and Brian's grandmother feel right now? Explain.

@ What is atonement? (At-one-ment). How can Scott atone for breaking the snow globe?

@ Tell about your most prized possession or about anything you have that once belonged to someone you love or loved?

@ What would you do if someone broke it or took it away from you?

Psalm 103:8-13
Proverbs 19:11

@ How exactly should Scott apologize to his grandmother? Why?

OUT OF THE COMFORT ZONE

Paul has almost never been out of the middle-class neighborhood where he grew up. The occasional family vacation stopped when his parents divorced. He still goes to visit his aunt and uncle in the next state every few years.

This year he is stretching himself spiritually and really committing to ministry and service. As part of this, he has traveled with his church youth group to the inner-city of Chicago on a mission trip. They are working in pairs at an apartment building for poverty level senior citizens.

Paul and one of the adult volunteers have been assigned to visit and clean the apartment of Mrs. Maxwell. She lives alone and is in a wheel chair. Her apartment is filthy. There is urine on the floor and she has placed all her soiled laundry in the tub. She hasn't bathed in some time.

Paul has never seen such filth. He thinks he is going to be sick. He is suddenly overwhelmed by the situation and rushes out into the hallway to escape the stench and the situation. The volunteer follows him out, places a hand on his shoulder and says, "Take a moment and then come back inside."

The adult goes back into the apartment, allowing Paul a moment to compose himself. Paul isn't so sure he'll go back inside to help.

DISCUSS:

@ **How far would you go to help someone? What is the personal line that you could not cross to help another? Explain.**

@ **What if God asked you to not just cross your personal line, but to leap over it?**

@ **How can a loving God permit people to live in squalor?**

@ **Do you think you would handle this challenge better or worse than Paul? Why?**

What's the most sacrificial act of service or ministry you've ever done?

Is saying, "It's not about our comfort. It's about showing Christ's love to Mrs. Maxwell" the whole truth...or too simplistic?

Should Paul go back in and help Mrs. Maxwell? Would you explain?

Read: **2 Thessalonians 1:11-12**
Romans 8:28
1 Peter 1:8-10, 19

If Paul doesn't go back in and help, how might his life and walk with God be impacted? If you were Paul... <u>how</u> would you make yourself go back in? Would it be difficult?

TAKE NOTES/MAKE NOTES

GETTING HIGH

Rachel is 16 and is on the perfect double date. She and her friend Laura are out with their boyfriends, Dan and Chuck. They, like Rachel and Laura, are best friends. The four of them went out to a nice restaurant. Then they went to a concert to hear a great band that all four of them liked.

Now as the evening winds down, Dan takes the four of them to his father's office building. He has arranged for the four of them to go onto the roof and look at the stars.

Rachel is terrified of heights. She does not even like to look out the second story window of her house. It is beyond a "slight" fear. When the fear comes upon her, she has been known to lose control and begin screaming. The date has been a dream up until now. As they step into the elevator, Rachel realizes what is happening and where they are going. Dan, Rachel's boyfriend, has never seen her freak out over heights. She fears she will lose him if he sees her freaking out. Panic shoots through her heart.

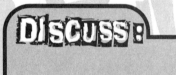 **DISCUSS:**

❧ **What is the difference between fear and cowardice?**

❧ **What is your biggest fear? How do you control it?**

❧ **Do you think Rachel is afraid of being on the roof or afraid of ruining a perfect date? Why?**

❧ **How is this situation about honesty and being transparent? Should she be honest with herself? With her friends? Explain.**

❧ **If Rachel freaks out...what would you say to her? If she doesn't, what would you say?**

 **Read:**

**Philippians 4:4-7; 2 Timothy 1:6
Philippians 4:6-7; Romans 2:12**

❧ **The elevator doors are about to open...pretend you are Rachel. What would you do next?**

LONG LOST FRIEND

Every student in Kim's school needs a certain amount of community service hours in order to graduate. The high school guidance counselor has set her up at the local "soup kitchen" to get the hours she needs. Kim is initially turned off, hoping for something a little "cleaner."

In spite of her initial hesitation, Kim shows up and does a pretty good job on her first day. She is actually having a good time and feeling good about what she is doing. She works hard and is friendly to everyone.

As she stands at the serving table, she looks up to see a familiar face down the line. It is her best friend from elementary school, a girl named Faith. They were inseparable. She and Kim lost contact when they went to separate middle schools.

Faith is thin, haggard and wearing raggedy clothes. She is also balancing a baby on her hip on one side while holding her plate with the other. In a moment she will be in front of Kim. Kim isn't sure she can face her. Kim is very uncomfortable. Faith looks homeless and Kim doesn't want to make her feel uncomfortable. She doesn't know what to say or do and is thinking of leaving.

@ **Should Kim feel guilty? Would you? Why?**

@ **Have you ever heard the phrase, "there, but for the grace of God, go I"? What does it mean?**

@ **Is it possible that this "chance" meeting wasn't chance at all? Why?**

@ **Do we get what we deserve? Explain.**

@ **Why might Kim be hesitant to face Faith and unsure what to do or say?**

@ **Do you think this is a "chance" meeting or not? Why?**

Philippians 2:1-5; James 1:2-4; 1 Peter 1:5-8; Luke 22:27

@ **How would you react if you were Kim?**

@ **Should Kim risk saying or doing the wrong thing to show love to Faith—or play it safe and leave? Explain.**

THE SCOOP

Todd is a reporter for his school paper. He writes a lot of stories about the school board and does teacher interviews, but he's always wanted to do something bigger.

One of last summer's biggest blockbuster movies (a film Todd loved) co-starred a former student of his school. The entertainment reporters are saying the man will be the "next big thing in Hollywood." His family still lives in the area.

On Thanksgiving weekend Todd looked up the family in the phone book hoping the "next big thing in Hollywood" would be home for Thanksgiving. He was. Scott asked for an interview and the star agreed.

The next day, he waited for the star for an hour at the back table of a diner. He finally showed up. He sat down and said simply, "let's get this over with." For the next 45 minutes, he trashed the town, the school, and even Todd (for calling his family's home on a holiday weekend). He made it clear he did not like Todd's clothes, his haircut, his interviewing style or anything else.

Todd left the interview apologizing profusely to the star and thanking him for his time, though he was crushed.

The next week, word spreads that Todd scored the big interview. The teacher that acts as a newspaper editor says she can't wait to read the interview and has promised page one.

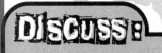

DISCUSS:

✺ **Tell us of a time when you were let down by a hero. How did that feel?**

✺ **Why do we build up our heroes to be more than human?**

✺ **Why is image important to us?**

✺ **Does "truth hurt"? Should it? Explain.**

If we do have a negative encounter with a celebrity we admire…should we let it bug us? Why? Should we respond in any way? Explain.

If you were Todd's friend and he told you about this experience, what would you say to him? Why?

Would you "spin" the story in a way so that you can get page one?

What should he tell his editor?

Read: 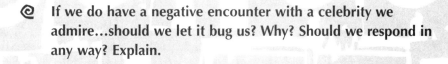 I Timothy 4:12
Joshua 24:15
Matthew 5:11-12

What should Todd do? (A "trash the hero" story? Find some good in what he got? Change the facts to make the interview seem more positive?) Explain.

What kind of story would you write if you were Todd? Why?

TAKE NOTES/MAKE NOTES

MY SISTER'S KEEPER

Cheryl has been on that border between the "popular crowd" and the "common geeks" the entire school year. She's been invited to more parties than ever; been invited to the lunch tables where the popular students sit; experienced a kind of makeover when she had her braces removed and got contacts. She's been the right amount of funny and given the right amount of attitude to nearly win a permanent place in the select group of "cool" people.

So taking her little sister to the mall was not how she wanted to spend a Saturday, but her parents both had to work. Cheryl's sister needed a whole list of items for school and has shown no signs of stopping or appreciation. Still Cheryl is having a better time than she thought she would have.

While at the mall Cheryl meets three of the girls from her lunch table. They look from her to her sister a few times and then invite Cheryl to join them at the café in the food court but "little sis" will have to sit someplace else. It's always the same with this new crowd, Cheryl has to change or give up something to hang with them. Cheryl looks at her sister and suddenly sees herself just a few years ago-braces, glasses, a bad haircut, and a favorite t-shirt with a tear and a stain-and her sister couldn't care less what the crowd thinks.

Cheryl looks at her sister and suddenly sees herself just a few years ago. Braces, glasses, and a bad haircut, Cheryl knows exactly what her younger sister is thinking and feeling

TAKE NOTES/MAKE NOTES

@ What crowd do you mostly hang out with? Why?

@ People may change the way they dress, or the language they use to be accepted—is there any amount of change that's worth it? Explain.

@ What do you think Cheryl is going through inside? What is her conflict?

@ If you have to change so much and work so hard to feel you belong to a certain crowd—is it worth it? Why?

@ If Cheryl went through what her sister is going through…what did she learn from that experience? Why?

@ What is the upside of "improving" yourself to fit in with a crowd? The downside?

@ What is the upside just being yourself and people accepting you for who you are? Any downside?

@ Can you think of something you always wanted and then, when you got it, you found out it wasn't worth what you had to give up? Tell us about it.

**2 Corinthians 6:4-6;
Colossians 3:13-14
Ephesians 4:29-32
2 Timothy 2:15**

@ If you were Cheryl, what would you do in this situation? Why?

@ What should Cheryl say to the girls in the mall?

JOYFUL NOISE

Dwight cannot sing very well. The problem is that Dwight loves to sing and what he lacks in natural talent, he makes up for in volume and enthusiasm. Though any member of the choir will tell you that Dwight is the weakest singer in the lot, they will also tell you he is probably the most liked, because of his humor, upbeat attitude, and the way he befriends any and all.

Dwight is in the 9th grade and is a part of the high school choir—the choir that has gone to state competitions for the last seven years and never achieved less than a stellar rating. One of the senior girls even told him that maybe he should just move his lips for the good of everyone.

The district competitions are in three weeks. If they don't get a perfect score there, they won't even get near the state level.

Mr. Davenport, the former music teacher, had no qualms about asking those who weren't up to the task to stay behind. The new teacher, Mrs. Praetorius, believes everybody should get to go.

Some of the seniors who've been in the choir for four years don't want to go out with a bad score. They've begun to glare at Dwight as he sings. One of the girls even told him that maybe he should just "move his lips for the good of everyone."

The district competitions are in three weeks. If they don't get a perfect score there, they won't even get near the state level.

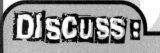

DISCUSS:

@ **Is this a story about self-sacrifice or self-acceptance? Explain.**

@ **Is this situation more about Dwight's self-sacrifice, or the choir having a more accepting attitude? Explain.**

@ **What happens when you eliminate the ingredients you don't like from the recipe? Explain.**

@ Who needs to be more understanding here? Why?

@ If we kick out one person for being less than perfect...what happens to us? Explain.

@ Do the needs of the group outweigh the needs of the one? Why?

@ If the choir is successful in talking Dwight out of going to the competition for being less than perfect, will that be good or bad for the choir in the long-term? Why?

Read: Ephesians 4:1-3
2 Corinthians 6:4-5
Philippians 3:12-14
Psalm 139

@ The concert is in one week. If you were Dwight, what would you do?

@ If you were a member of the choir, what would you do?

TAKE NOTES/MAKE NOTES

THE REPORT CARD

Marc's had a bad year—at least academically. He's made the A/B Honor Roll ever since junior high, but not this year. This year, he has just fizzled out. He has no desire to excel and do his best.

Whereas in previous years he couldn't wait to go to school, this year he could care less about any of it—and it shows in his work. His most recent report card has three "D"s.

He hasn't told his parents about his trouble—he just knows they would ground him from computer, soccer…everything.

As far as they know, things have been as good this year as they have been in the past. He's even lied to them a few times about how good he is doing (hoping he would be able to pull his grades up through some last-minute miracle).

Now he is riding his bike home from school. In his backpack, in a sealed envelope, is his rancid report card—along with a formal request for Marc's parents to make an appointment for a parent/teacher conference.

TAKE NOTES/MAKE NOTES

DISCUSS:

@ Did Marc lie by not letting his parents know he is struggling in school? Explain.

@ Why do you think Marc is trying to cover this up—what's the thought process?

@ What happens when you keep news like this to yourself? Why?

@ How long can you hide bad news?

@ Do things generally get better when you hide them from parents...or worse? Give an example.

@ What do you think of Marc's approach? Why?

@ How do you think it will end with Marc and his parents? What do you think he will go through as a result of being dishonest? Explain.

@ If Marc had chosen to be honest with his parents from the start, how might things ended differently? What problems and pain would he have avoided? Explain.

@ If you were Marc's parents, how would you punish him, if at all?

Read:

Psalm 51:6-9
Luke 16:10-12
Hebrews 12:11

@ In light of our discussion and this passage...what should Marc's next move be?

TAKE NOTES/MAKE NOTES

HONESTY, SCHOOL, MOTIVATION

ACROSS THE BOARD

Travis has been a member of his youth group since junior high. He showed up every Sunday. At first it was because his parents made him attend.

Then as he got older, he liked going, but for purely social reasons, nothing spiritual. He's never "felt" what others say they "feel" when they worship together or watch the sunrise at the end of a lock-in.

Two weeks ago Travis was in his room and said aloud to God (or his ceiling) "If you are really there, then give me a sign."

The next morning, on the way to school, Travis noticed the telephone poles looked like crosses. He'd never noticed that before, but he put it out of his mind.

At a stop light he noticed the man in the car next to him had a cross tattoo on his arm. When his teacher erased the board, she left a huge cross shape in the dust. The girl with the locker next to his wore a cross earring.

Now, everywhere he looks he sees crosses. He's not trying to. If fact he doesn't want to see them at all, but for the last two weeks everywhere he looks he sees the shape.

Travis believes he is either going crazy, or...God is talking to him.

TAKE NOTES/MAKE NOTES

DISCUSS:

@ Do you think God is speaking to Travis? Why?

@ How does God talk to folks in the Bible?

@ How would you like God to talk to you? Why? About what?

@ Are people crazy who believe God speaks to them? Why?

@ All the crosses he is seeing were probably there long before he started noticing, so why would he suddenly notice them?

@ What might God be saying to Travis by helping him notice all these crosses?

@ Could God talk to one person through a "sign" seen by many people?

 **Read:**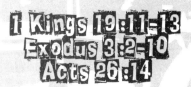

1 Kings 19:11-13
Exodus 3:2-10
Acts 26:14

@ Name all the ways you believe God speaks to people. When do you think God might have spoken to you? Explain.

@ If you were Travis how would you bring the subject up to someone? Who would you tell?

TAKE NOTES/MAKE NOTES

HEARING GOD, SUPERNATURAL, RELATIONSHIP WITH GOD

THE JERK

Molly is hopelessly in love with Mitchell. She writes his name on all her notebooks. She talks about him and her love for him all the time to her friends. She stays on the phone with him until her mother has to yank the phone from her hand. She has a page in her school notebook filled with her first name next to his last name. She has never been happier.

Paula is Molly's best friend and she thinks Mitch is a jerk. He never does the actual calling—Molly calls him. He ignores her when he's with his friends, fails to pick her up when he says he's going to, makes fun of her in front of others, flirts with other girls right in front of her, and makes her pay for dates when he says he "forgot" his wallet.

Paula wants her friend to be happy but more and more she finds herself keeping a list of all the ways that Mitch doesn't respect Molly. Molly seems so blinded to Mitch's bad side that Paula is praying to uncover something "big" enough to finally get her attention—so Molly can see he is a jerk and dump him fast.

- Is any of this Paula's business? Why?

- What do you think of Paula's campaign to expose Mitch and show Molly who he really is? Should she just butt out? Why?

- Is the person with the problem always the last one to see it? Why?

- Even if she isn't seeing Mitch clearly, if Molly is happy, what's the problem?

- Have you had anyone worm their way into the middle of any of your relationships? What happened?

- In your opinion, with what you know about Mitch, is he good or bad for Molly? Why?

Read: **1 Corinthians 13:4-7**
Philippians 2:3-4
Matthew 7:1

- If you were close to Molly (like Paula) would you consider it more loving for her to get involved or just stay out of Molly's business? Why?

- What would say to Molly if you were Paula?

GOD CALLING

Geoff considers himself just an everyday teenager. He maintains pretty good grades. He mows lawns to make extra money. He (probably) spends too much time playing video games. He likes science fiction movies and swimming.

He never thought there was all that much special about him. There were certainly other kids in his school he would say were better than he was at most things.

Geoff was asked by his youth minister to read the scripture and give a five-minute sermon on it for Youth Sunday. In this, he was the best. His message had a huge impact on the people. Many crowded around him and complimented him afterwards. This surprised Geoff.

He's always enjoyed the Bible, and speaking about it in his easy, humorous, engaging way, but he never thought he possessed any special talent or skill in it. The senior pastor, in his 70's, told Geoff privately that he should really think about being a pastor.

@ How do you know what God's calling is for your life? How do you know if God is calling you?

@ How are we to discover our calling? Are we to hear God alone on what our calling is, or can others help us pinpoint it? Explain.

@ Do you think that your calling will tie in at least a little bit with what you want to do with your life? Do you think it matters to God what YOU want? Should it? Why?

Romans 8:28-30
Mark 2:17
1 Corinthians 7:17
Colossians 3:23

@ How can Geoff know his calling?

@ What would you do if you were Geoff? Why?

CALLING, MINISTRY, TALENTS

NOT AMUSED

Every year the eighth grade class gets to spend a day at a nearby amusement park. It is the last "big deal" before summer and the class will start a new year at the "high school building." Erin is hanging out with a small group of friends. They are laughing and talking about what it will be like to be "freshmen" next year. The fear on Erin's mind is that she will never see her old friends and will be ignored by the high school students.

The group decides to go for the new tallest-fastest roller coaster in the park for their first ride of the day. The line for the new roller coaster is two hours long. When their turn comes, they discover they have an odd number of riders. Erin volunteers to wait for the next train.

Erin waves to her friends as they disappear. She rides the next train alone. It isn't near as much fun as riding with someone else. When she gets off the ride, the group is nowhere to be found. Erin looks around and even wanders over to the ride entrance to see if they got back in line, but they are not there. She waits for ten minutes to see if they notice she's not in the group, but no one returns for her. She is pretty crushed.

DISCUSS:

- Have you ever been "ditched" by a group like this? Is that what happened here (or could it just be a careless mistake)? Explain.

- Make an analogy between what's happened to Erin and life as a teenager—especially one going from junior high to high school.

- Three questions to answer at once: Do you like to be alone? Could you live by yourself? Go do a movie by yourself? Why?

- What are Erin's options at this point?

Read:

I Corinthians 13:4-7
Proverbs 27:10; Romans 14:5-7
Luke 5:16; Philippians 4:12-13

- What should Erin do or say when she eventually hooks up with her friends?

WHERE THERE'S SMOKE

Mrs. Anderson, Gwen's third period teacher, has a habit of walking out in the middle of class. She will typically declare, "study break" and put someone in charge when she leaves. Most students know she's going for a cigarette in the teacher's lounge and everyone simply clowns around until she returns.

During a recent test, Mrs. Anderson said, "Gwen, you're in charge" and walked out. She wasn't out of the room for two minutes when someone said, "What did anybody get for number 2?"

Someone else said, "B" out loud. Soon everyone was trading answers. Several minutes later, Mrs. Anderson walks back into the room smelling of smoke and asks jokingly, "Well, Gwen...did anyone cheat while I was gone"?

@ Is cheating acceptable under any circumstance—even if as a result of an adult shirking her responsibility? Explain.

@ If you cheat and get caught, whose fault is it? Why?

@ Is this a case of "all's fair in love and war"? Why?

@ Is there any answer that Gwen can give that won't get her in trouble? If yes, what is it?

@ If Gwen answers truthfully, what will happen? If she doesn't, what will happen?

@ Is there any answer Gwen can give that won't get her in trouble? What is it?

Ephesians 5:8-11
Proverbs 11:12
Proverbs 10:19
Joshua 24:15

@ What would you do if you were Gwen?

SHATTERED

Lana lives in an apartment building. One day, when she was bored out of her skull, Lana got with the older girl across the hall and they found a way to get out onto the roof of their building.

After being up there a few minutes, the girls were bored. They made paper airplanes and sent them flying over the edge.

Last Saturday, Lana and her friend were on the roof again. They soon ran out of airplanes and began looking around for other things to throw. They found stones and bits of gravel and threw those over. The neighbor girl tossed over a broomstick she found.

Lana found a beer bottle and tossed it gently over the edge. Both girls heard the scream.

An elderly woman from the first floor was just leaving the building when Lana dropped the bottle. It didn't hit her but a piece of the glass went into the woman's eye. She had to go to the emergency room.

The police are questioning people in the building and will soon reach Lana's apartment as well as that of her friend across the hall. They can hear the police as they knock on doors closer and closer to theirs.

TAKE NOTES/MAKE NOTES

BOREDON, CRIME, MISTAKES

DISCUSS:

@ What happens when you try to hide something that could get you into trouble? Why?

@ Tell of a time when you did something bad, then tried to hide it and things got worse.

@ Have you ever "gotten away" with something bad? Any regrets about it or hiding it? Explain.

@ Do you think Lana and her friend are willing to come forward and admit what they've done or are they tempted to cover it up and admit nothing? Why?

@ How does guilt work? Explain?

@ How would Lana redeem herself? Why?

@ If the Bible says "Love does not keep a record of wrongs" and that "God is love"...does that mean that Lana is in the clear? Why?

@ What do you think God thinks of a life strategy of hiding bad things you do? What do you think God wants you to do when you do something bad, or make mistakes that hurt people? Why?

Read:

1 John 1:6-10
Proverbs 8:1-21
Ephesians 5:15
Romans 13:1-3

@ If the elderly woman is okay, how should Lana respond? If the woman is injured permanently, how should Lana respond? If Lana is "walking in the light," shouldn't she respond the same whether the elderly woman was hurt badly or not? Why?

@ What should the next sentence out of Lana's mouth be?

FACE TIME

Becky is in a beauty pageant. She's won several pageants since she was a little girl. Now, in the eleventh grade, she's still entering them.

Becky's also done a few modeling jobs…just little ones…for several catalogues and a small magazine. Everyone tells her that she could be a professional model. Her real dream is to design and build skyscrapers.

Becky has a friend named Debbie, one of her few "real" friends, who tells her "You're objectifying women—supporting the system that values women for their looks, not their brains. Your looks are being used to sell products. Don't settle for being superficial?"

Becky wants to know what is wrong with being pretty. If she doesn't get a scholarship through the pageants, she could earn money as a model for a few years and then go to college on a full ride if she plays her cards right.

- In magazines and catalogs you see, are the models pretty or "regular people"? Why?

  - What would happen if we looked at beauty as a talent like singing or writing?

  - If you were Becky, how would you feel? Is there anything wrong with being pretty? Explain.

- What do we teach our children when we hold up the "pretty" people as being somehow worth more than others? How do we change this?

- Do you agree with Becky's friend Debbie, that Becky is "objectifying women—supporting the system that values women for their looks, not their brains"? That Becky is superficial? Explain.

- Should Becky rethink her pageant and modeling strategy? Why?

  - Do you like to have your picture taken?

1 Samuel 16:7
Romans 12:6
2 Corinthians 12:7-10

- If you were Becky, how would you respond to Debbie? Why?

  - If you were Debbie where would you take the next step?

SMOKIN'

Jack smokes. His parents both smoke and they know that he does. He's never been caught at school and is careful not to smoke in front of people who don't like it. He understands what it's like to "need" a cigarette. Sometimes he just has to have one. To Jack this is no different than somebody else "needing" a cup of coffee.

Jack has been invited to go on a mission trip with a friend's church youth group. The youth minister has asked everyone who goes to sign an agreement before they leave that says they will not smoke, drink, get into other people's stuff—and a list of other "Don'ts". Jack explains to the youth minister that he smokes but he is discreet about it. He'll even provide a note from his parents that says they don't care if Jack smokes as long as he doesn't give them to other kids.

The youth minister says that if Jack wants to smoke, he can't go. He is welcome to go on the trip but if he is caught smoking his parents will have to drive nine hours to get him, regardless of what day or time it is.

@ **Is needing a cigarette any different from needing a "sugar buzz" or a "caffeine rush"? How so?**

@ **Define "addiction."**

@ **Is there an unfair stigma attached to smoking? Explain.**

@ **What's wrong with Jack smoking on the mission trip, if he has an okay from his parents and he promises to be discreet? Explain.**

I Corinthians 3:16-17
Romans 1:29-32
I Corinthians 3:16-17
John 8:7

@ **Jack has three choices: convince the youth pastor to change the rule for everybody; don't go on the mission trip, or; go on the missions trip and don't smoke. If you were Jack, what would you choose? Why?**

MAKING THE GRADE

Martha has never made good grades. She has always managed to get by with B's and C's and that's good enough for her. She never saw the point in breaking her neck to get A's and she has no aspiration to be an A student—in fact, she and her friends find A students to be irritating. Her parents accept the B's, tell her to work harder on the C's and pretty much let it go at that.

This is Martha's sophomore year. For some reason, things seem to come easier to her now. She started off the year with a series of stellar test scores. She found that hitting the books just a little bit every night has drastically improved her grades.

Martha's friends are not happy for her. They're calling Martha a nerd, and saying she thinks she's better than them—the same stuff they all used to say about A students. The A students still see her as a slacker and don't talk to her much outside of class. For the first time she has a real chance at straight A's on a report card but feels she has lost her friends in the process.

- Bottom line, are grades really important? Back up your answer. Why?

- What is Martha feeling right now? Tell of a time when you felt that way. How did you respond?

- Have you ever heard the phase "The only constant thing is change"? What does it mean?

- If you received a "D" on a test and your best friend scored an "A", would you congratulate him or her? Why?

- Why are Martha's friends reacting as they are to the change in her grades? Why are the "A" students reacting to her as they are?

- Both groups seem to want to keep Martha in a box. Is this fair? Why?

- Why do we have a tendency to put people in boxes? Explain.

 Proverbs 17:17

- What should Martha do?

RESTRICTED VIEWING

Paul and Colin are both 12 and are dying to see the new movie *Airborne*, starring their favorite action hero. They've seen all his videos. No one seems to care that the movies are rated "R." The video store rents "R" videos to anyone, and their parents only roll their eyes at the language, violence and brief nudity, but have never told either of the two that they can't watch the films.

Paul and Colin can't for the movie to come out on video, so they buy tickets for the "PG" movie and then sneak into the film they want to see. Halfway into the film the two feel a hand on their shoulder and an usher is asking them to leave. The manager is waiting at the exit and brings them into his office. They are told to call their parents to tell them what has happened and to be picked up.

- What's the problem with all this—anybody who has cable has heard the words and seen the blood anyway? Explain.

  - Was what Paul and Colin did dishonest, or were they in their rights since so many adults don't seem to care what they watch? Explain.

- Is the fact that Paul and Colin's parents don't apply any standards to what movies they watch, a good thing or a bad thing? Why?

- What would you do if you were Paul or Colin's parents? Why?

  - Think of Paul and Colin as Christians. What are some different choices they could have made and actions they could have taken to avoid this whole situation? Explain.

- How are movie ratings similar to laws? As Christians, should we obey them or disregard them? Explain.

  - Why is the rating system put in place? Why is there an age limit on drinking? On driving? Explain.

Read: Proverbs 1:1-7; Romans 13:1 James 3:10-12; James 1:4

- When Paul and Colin talk to their parents, what should they say? What should they do?

  - In the future, what should they change in respect to their movie viewing?

MOVIES, HONESTY, STANDARDS

KELLY GREEN

Dana wonders why her life is so hard and chaotic and why nothing comes easy for her. She works really hard to get good grades. Guys don't seem interested in her. If she wants to go to college, she'll pay her own way. If she wants a car, she'll have to buy it herself.

It seems like her family is always immersed in some family crisis—accidents, illness, arguments and more. Life just doesn't seem fair.

She's not just being jealous. For example, there is a girl in her class named Kelly. Kelly gets straight A's effortlessly. Kelly has a cute boyfriend. Kelly's family has money, but on top of that, she has done modeling work and has plenty of her own money.

Kelly was promised a new car for her graduation gift. She can select the college of her choice. Her home life is harmonious and happy. Her life seems more than fair.

Dana has heard all the talk about being content with who you are and with what you have, but she just doesn't feel it.

- Is life fair? Support your thinking on this.
  - Who do you know who is like Dana? Like Kelly? (No names!)
  - Who are you more like, Dana or her friend Kelly? Explain.
- Do the people who "have it all" truly have it all? Explain.
  - Do you appreciate the A you were handed or the one you worked for?
  - Is Dana dealing with jealously or unfairness? Explain.
- What is the upside of things coming easy in life? The downside? The upside of things coming hard in life? The downside?
  - What does it mean to be content?
  - What's the hard part of "great is your reward in heaven"?

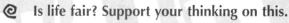

Read:
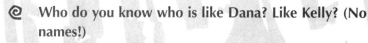
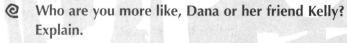
Philippians 4:12-13
Psalm 63
Ecclesiastes 9:11
1 Corinthians 2:25
Isaiah 11:3-4

- Is it possible or impossible for Dana to find contentment in her life? Explain. What would you do if you were Dana? Why?

YOUR "BOY" IS BACK IN TOWN

Two years ago Andrew was at his worst. He and his friend Brent were constantly in trouble. They were in a few fights. They shoplifted. They were experimenting with drugs and cutting class. Neither one cared about his grades. Several times they were returned home by police after sneaking out and hanging out on the street. Ultimately they were both expelled from school.

When Brent "borrowed" a friend's car for a joyride, he wound up going to a juvenile detention center for a year. At that point, Brent and Andrew parted ways and haven't talked since.

It's been a great year for Andrew. He started taking school seriously and found he could make great grades. Without Brent around to talk trash to folks and start fights, Andrew hasn't fought anyone in a whole year. He's done no drugs. He's become a part of a cool local church youth group. He's getting along with his parents. Now the only notes his parents get from school are compliments and praise for Andrew's outstanding academic performance.

Today Andrew received a post card from Brent stating that he would be out soon and couldn't wait to get together for some fun. Andrew isn't sure it's a good idea to hang around Brent again.

DISCUSS:

@ **Have you ever royally screwed up a relationship, but then were able to put it back together? Tell us what happened.**

> @ **How long does it take to earn back someone's trust after you've wrecked it?**

> @ **Have you ever had to break off a friendship that wasn't healthy? Why?**

@ **Does Andrew have an obligation to Brent to try and help him? To just pick up where they left off? Why?**

@ **What is Andrew going through? Why?**

> @ **Just as Superman must stay away from kryptonite...are there some people who are just "kryptonite" to our lives whom we should stay away from? Explain.**

@ **Tell about a time when you had to break off a friendship that wasn't healthy.**

> @ **Would it be a good idea for Andrew to hang with Brent and try to influence him for good? Why?**

Read: **1 Corinthians 15:33; Ephesians 4:14 Philippians 4:11-13; Matthew 13:3-9 Proverbs 17:17; Proverbs 13:20**

@ **In light of this verse, should Andrew get with Brent or not? Why?**

YOUR "BOY" IS BACK IN TOWN PART 2

Brent "borrowed" a friend's car for a joyride, was caught by the police, and wound up in the juvenile detention center for a year. He had one friend in high school, Andrew, that used to hang out with him and "get in trouble" with him. Andrew was not part of the car "borrowing" but Brent was on his way to pick Andrew up when he was caught.

Brent is hoping things can be like old times when he gets out soon. He sent a letter to Andrew but he hasn't heard back yet. He will soon be getting out and his parents have already given him a list of their "requirements" if he is to move back in with them and finish high school.

Brent feels real pressure to be different, but doubts he can change—too much fun living like he's always lived. To hear his parents tell it, Andrew has become a "saint" which only adds to his pressure. For a moment, the ideas of a second chance, a fresh start, and of being a good person really appeals to him. But then he just laughs it off, "too late for me," he decides.

DISCUSS:

@ How expensive is forgiveness? Explain.

@ Is it possible to leave your past behind you and start over? Is it painful? Is it free?

@ Is it ever too late to find a new start,

@ Why is it so hard for us to believe that God can forgive any of us for anything? Explain.

@ Is it easy or difficult for you to believe that someone like Brent can find Christ? Why?

@ What do you predict for the future of Andrew and Brent's friendship? Why?

@ What's the most you've ever forgiven someone? Why?

@ What's the most you've ever been forgiven?

Read:
Psalm 103:11-12
2 Corinthians 5:17
1 Corinthians 13:5
James 5:10-12

@ What should Brent do?

WHAT YOU WISH FOR

After what seems like a lifetime of living in the shadow of her sister, Millie feels like she has finally come into her own. Millie's sister is two years older than she is and it seems like Millie gets stuck with all the same teachers her sister had. These teachers all insist on comparing the two. To hear them tell it, Millie's sister was an angel straight from heaven, a perfect student.

Fortunately, the school has a new math teacher, Mr. Jeffers-the first teacher that Millie has that did not have her sister also. Mr. Jeffers has started a club for students who want to compete against other schools. She doesn't think about it very much, she just joins. Millie has always made good grades in math, but nothing outstanding. It is her first chance to do something that her sister didn't do, and Millie thinks she can shine.

Almost immediately Millie's good feelings disappear. The club is nothing but hard work. The "class brains" in the club act as though they could enter the competition with one brain tied behind their backs. Millie doesn't want to quit but she feels like she traded one set of problems for another.

@ **Have you ever been in someone else's shadow? Whose and why?**

> @ **If "all the world is a stage" would you be center stage, back stage or in the audience? Where do you want to be?**
>
> @ **Did Millie make a mistake? How?**

@ **Why did Millie join the math club? Was that the right reason? Explain.**

> @ **How would you have reacted, had you faced the constant comparisons that Millie endured? Why?**

@ **What comes easy for you? What's your best subject?**

@ **Did Millie join the math club for the right reasons? Explain.**

Romans 12:4-8; James 1:2-4 Luke 15:28-30; 1 Corinthians 7:7

@ **Did Millie make a mistake? Explain. What should she do now?**

PACKING HEAT?

Rose and Gail have known each other since Gail moved to town in the 7th grade. They are not related, but they have the same last name so they always sit near each other in class. Even their lockers are side by side.

One day, Rose was sure she saw a gun in Gail's locker. She only caught a glimpse but couldn't be sure. She went discreetly to a teacher and told her what she thought she saw. The teacher panicked and had the hallway sealed off. For an hour the principal and senior staffers conducted an inspection of all the lockers.

The gun turned out to be a curling iron. Administrators found a number of things, in other lockers, including drugs, so police and parents were called on a number of students. Some students were grateful for the disruption that caused cancellation of scheduled tests. Many students were upset about the invasion of privacy.

One girl was mortified when it was discovered she had a picture of a boy she liked in her locker. Everyone is looking at Rose as a snitch, fink, tattle-tale (you pick your favorite word).

Students who overheard the first teacher and principal talking, quickly discovered Rose made the call. Gail won't talk to her now and many students are really mad at her.

Others jokingly refer to her as the school "undercover" detective ("Hey Rose...Jimmy is over here sexually harassing me...turn him in too!").

Rose wonders if she'll ever live this down.

DISCUSS:

    © **Did Rose do anything wrong? Could she have done anything differently? Explain.**

    © **Have you ever known something that could get someone else into trouble but said nothing? What happened?**

    © **Tell of a time when you knew something bad was going to happen or you knew someone had done something bad. Did you tell or keep it to yourself? Why?**

Should Rose have spoken to Gail first? Where do loyalties belong when you think you discover something really bad? Discuss.

Some say to never tell on somebody else…for any reason. Do you agree with this? Why?

Some people live in pain rather than say something to someone in authority. How would you make it easier for someone in pain to come forward and get help in your school?

 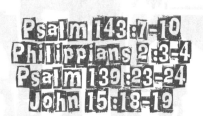

Psalm 143:7-10
Philippians 2:3-4
Psalm 139:23-24
John 15:18-19

If you were Rose what would you do to live this down, put it behind you, or to try and restore your friendship with Gail?

TAKE NOTES/MAKE NOTES

THE MORNING AFTER

Ross has three friends who seem to be forever on the verge of trouble. They all have a great sense of humor and the group of them get together and share the same opinions on bands, movies, girls, and the futility of high school.

Mike is the loudest of the group and recently said that he had this great idea for how to "thank" the school for all it had done for them. The four of them agree to meet behind the school the next night. All of them meet, except Ross, whose mother asked him to help her with some boxes at the last minute.

The morning after, Ross enters the school and sees the damage. Profanity of all kinds has been spray painted on the walls. Lockers are damaged. The trophy case has been smashed open and the trophies stolen.

The computer lab (Ross' favorite subject) has been broken into and the equipment trashed or missing. The idea seemed funny two days ago, but now, seeing the full impact of the damage, he is ashamed to have even been part of planning it.

The administration is in chaos. To replace the equipment in the lab will set the class back by three months and Ross may end up having to make up the work in Summer school. Mike passed Ross in the hall on the way to the all-school assembly and simply gave Ross a quick wink and a smile.

A special assembly is announced, and teachers go to the microphones and list all the damage detail by detail. Then the principal asks any students responsible or with knowledge, to come forward.

TAKE NOTES/MAKE NOTES

 **DISCUSS:**

@ Would you remain friends with these friends? Why?

@ What do you think of what Ross' friends did to the school?

@ If you were one of the ones who wrecked the school and someone turned you in, would you stay friends with Ross? Why?

@ Why do you think some people take pleasure in ruining things for others? Is this a big deal? Explain.

@ What is Ross's responsibility to the school? To his friends? Explain.

@ Is there ever a time to turn friends in for something like this or do you maintain code of silence no matter what? Explain.

Why does it seem some people always feel like the victim?
@ If it was you, how could you justify what happened?

@ Why do you think some people take pleasure in ruining things for others? Is this a big deal?

 **Read:**

**Proverbs 3:29-33
Isaiah 59:14-15
Romans 12:17-18**

@ Complete this sentence "Ross should…"

TAKE NOTES/MAKE NOTES

MAKING THE GRADE

Many students in Mr. Langer's history class wonder how he made it to being a teacher. He is seldom prepared. The homework he assigns is never returned and sometimes lost. Students can't figure out how he arrives at the grades he puts at the top of their papers.

Amy has been pulling straight A's all year. After a disastrous year in 8th grade she is finally doing well. Mr. Langer has given her a 76 percent on the last two tests with no other marks on the paper. She's talked to a few friends and it seems like Mr. Langer is handing out grades randomly. Amy knew she probably didn't deserve the 76 on the first test. (She deserved much lower.) But she studied hard for the second test and feels she should have gotten a better grade.

@ How is this an honesty issue?

@ If you were getting straight 92's and someone let the teacher know she had made an error (causing you to get a lower grade), what would you do? Why?

@ Would you rather have a hard-earned B or a dishonest A? Explain.

@ Tell of a teacher you've had like Mr. Langer. In general, what is the best approach toward such teachers? Why?

@ Have you ever gotten too much change from a clerk? Did you give it back?

@ If a teacher is incompetent, is it okay to cheat in their class or to be disrespectful? Should you challenge or go along with their incompetence—like choose not to challenge them when they lose your homework? Explain.

James 1:2-5
Romans 5:2-5
James 1:5-6
1 Corinthians 6:12

@ Should Amy play this to her advantage? Should she challenge Mr. Langer or just let this all slide and hope for the best? Explain.

MISSED IT BY THAT MUCH

Tom and Scott have been friends for a while now. Tom is a brain and Scott is an artist. They both play in the high school band and belong to the Spanish club. Scott gets extra credit in his history class by creating murals for his teacher to hang on the wall of the classroom.

He has done this all year, working mostly after school. The teacher trusts Scott, and leaves most days simply asking him to lock the door before he leaves.

One afternoon Scott is working on yet another mural. Tom is sitting at the teacher's desk, just hanging out. Tom finds the teacher's grade book and begins to peruse.

He spots a quiz Scott bombed a few weeks ago, scoring a 38%. The teacher's red pen is attached to the book. Tom offers to change Tom's grade to an 88%. Scott knows he is on the line between a C and a B so far this semester.

Discuss:

@ **What's the harm if Tom changes Scott's grade—it's just one grade?**

@ **If integrity is defined as "the kind of person you are when no one is looking," what kind of integrity does Scott have? Tom? You?**

@ **If you tell a lie and no one finds out, does it hurt anything? Explain.**

@ **Scott has earned a certain amount of trust from his teacher. Even if she never finds out about the grade change, how would that trust be violated if he lets Tom change it as offered?**

Read: **Proverbs 20:9-11**
Philippians 2:12-13
2 Timothy 2:15
1 Corinthians 10:13

@ **Tom's best course of action is...**

@ **Scott's best course of action is...**

CHEATING, HONESTY, TRUST

KEEPING WARM

Ben is on a mission trip with his church youth group. He read all the forms and papers, but he really doesn't know what to expect. This is his first mission trip.

The group is working in the hills of West Virginia. They are to spend the week working to help a man "winterize" his house. They are to add insulation, fix windows, and do other difficult jobs.

Ben cannot believe the poverty he sees. The man's home is a wreck. It appears he hasn't done anything to improve his own home in years. He seems perfectly capable to Ben. Yet he just sits on his porch all day and watches the group work. He doesn't even help them clean the trash out of his yard.

Ben finds himself getting angrier and angrier as the week goes on. Here they are working their butts off and the homeowner does nothing to pitch in and hasn't even given a simple "Thank You."

DISCUSS:

© What is the point of mission work? Why do it? Explain.

© Why is it harder to do something for someone who is ungrateful?

© Is mission work about us or the people we serve doing it? If it is about the people we serve, then why does it make a difference whether they thank us or not?

© Is this a case of "you made your own bed, now lay in it"? Explain.

© What is "unconditional" love? What is "agape"? How does that apply to this situation? Explain.

© Jesus said, "Feed my sheep" Did he put any "if" or "as long as" on the statement?

Read:

1 Corinthians 13:2-3
John 21:15-17
Ephesians 2:19-22
2 Corinthians 12:15

© What would you do if you were Ben? Why?

A FAMILY ADDITION

Claire and her brother Benny have always been like best friends. They were there for each other when their father died five years ago. They supported each other through the worst times and have always confided in each other about everything.

Claire is now a senior in high school and Benny graduated from college last summer. In November, Benny e-mails Claire to tell the family that he will be home for Christmas with a big surprise.

A few days before Christmas, Claire's brother arrives at his parents' home...with his new wife.

His wife has a 2-year-old daughter she had on her own. Claire's mother is distraught, but is an expert at putting on a happy face, so welcomes her son's family warmly. Claire is nice to them, but ends up spending as much time as she can in her room—away from her brother and his new family.

Claire finds herself crying uncontrollably...but she doesn't know why.

@ **What is Claire going through? Why?**

@ **How would you feel if a close family member made a major life decision and didn't tell you or anyone? Why?**

@ **Is it anybody else's business?**

@ **Which do you think is most upsetting to Claire: that her brother got married or for not telling her he was getting married? Why?**

@ **What has changed in Claire and her brother's relationship? Why?**

Colossians 3:13
Galatians 6:2-5

@ **What should Claire say to her brother? To her mother?**

LITTLE LIES

Theresa and Shelia met at the beginning of the year and have become good friends. They trade earrings and secrets and often study together at one another's homes.

Theresa is at Shelia's house when the phone rings. Shelia answers and makes a face. She looks a Theresa and mouths the words "Walter Cubbins," Walter Cubbins will never make the popular list.

He's called to ask Shelia out. Shelia asks him to slow down and calm down because he is so nervous. Theresa thinks that's cute.

Theresa hears Shelia say, "I can't. I'm going to be out of town, on a trip with Theresa. I'm sorry." Shelia has just lied three times effortlessly—and involved Theresa in the lie (now she has to remember which weekend, where they went, what they did...in case asked about it later by Walter or anyone else).

And she lied to Walter, who may not be popular, but who is sweet and could use a friend. Shelia puts down the phone and says, "Ooooooooo...ick!" and goes back to her studying.

Theresa just stares at Shelia, hoping her friend will notice her concern and talk about this. She wants to say something herself, but is astonished that her friend is so casual about it.

Is a lie a lie no matter what? Explain.

Was Shelia protecting Walter's feelings or her own? Why?

People use little white lies all the time. What's the big deal for Theresa about Shelia doing it?

What do you think of Shelia's approach to Walter's invitation? Explain.

How could Shelia have treated Walter with a little more love and respect?

@ How could Sheila have treated Theresa with a little more love and respect?

@ What is the price of popularity? What do you pay to get it and what do you pay once you have it?

@ Is it worth it to be popular when it means rejecting other people or withholding friendship from them? Why?

Read: Ephesians 4 :22-25
1 Samuel 16:7
Luke 6 :32-34

@ What would you do if you were Theresa? If you were Walter and found out?

@ Should she challenge Shelia on any of this? How? Why?

TAKE NOTES/MAKE NOTES

OUT WITH A BANG

Mark has three friends he's known since elementary school. They have always done stuff together. They've pulled a few pranks on their teachers and various neighbors but never anything more serious than soaping windows or posting signs on the back of teachers' cars.

Mark's dad bought him six M-80's (a very powerful firecracker). He takes them with him when he meets with the guys. One of the guys, Jamie, takes an M-80 from Mark. He thinks it would be cool to use it on Mrs. Anderson's mailbox to "see what will happen,"

None of the boys like Mrs. Anderson. She is an elderly woman who always complains when they cut through her yard on their way home from school.

The boys sneak out at night and over to her house. The M-80 explodes and blows the mailbox right off the post. It lands on top of Mrs. Anderson's car. The boys did not imagine this would happen. They decide to run away.

Within minutes, the police arrive at Mrs. Anderson's home. A half hour later there is a policeman at Mark's front door. They talk about the firecracker, the (fromer) mail box, the damaged car, the threat of fire, the shock to Mrs. Anderson, and...on and on. His parents stand there looking at him. Mark looks from one to the other and to the policeman.

TAKE NOTES/MAKE NOTES

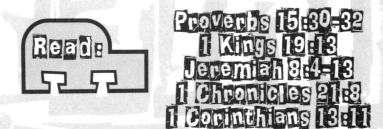

VANDALISM, HONESTY, BETRAYAL

DISCUSS:

ⓔ What counts as being "an accident"? Does this count? Why?

ⓔ Would you keep your mouth shut, no matter what? Even if it meant you get in trouble instead of your guilty friends? Explain.

ⓔ Have you ever heard the phrase "it's all fun and games until someone loses an eye"? Is it true?

ⓔ What could these guys have done to avoid this whole situation?

ⓔ Mark is not sure how to respond. Should he keep his mouth shut, no matter what or be honest?

ⓔ If it gets his friends in trouble, should Mark still tell the truth? If it gets his dad in trouble (for buying the M-80's for him), should he still tell the truth? Why?

ⓔ Do actions have re-actions? Give an example.

ⓔ What happens when stupidity is followed by more stupidity? How hard is it to do what is right? Explain.

Read:
Proverbs 15:30-32
1 Kings 19:13
Jeremiah 8:4-13
1 Chronicles 21:8
1 Corinthians 13:11

ⓔ What's the right thing Mark should do? Why?

TAKE NOTES/MAKE NOTES

VALUES? WHAT VALUES?

Richard has been in the band since the 7th grade. He's been invited to a party (Technically, the whole band was invited). It's a big house. There are probably 45 or 50 students at the party and no adults.

A few kids snuck in alcohol, but most don't bother. Richard is talking to the people he knows well and avoiding the popular crowd.

One of the flag girls all the guys have been ogling has had too much to drink. Giggling, she comes over to Richard and says, "Come with me." Richard shyly follows her to the back bedroom of the house.

She switches the light off and immediately starts kissing him. He can taste the beer. She lifts his hands toward her breasts and says, "Do what you want to do."

DISCUSS:

    ◐ If Richard just does a little, but doesn't go all the way, is there any problem? Why?

    ◐ After all the classes and books and discussions...what is really going to help when it comes time to make the big decision whether or not to have sex? Explain.

    ◐ Is the best time to make this decision for or against sex when you are at a party with a willing, drunk person? Why?

    ◐ When should we make the important decisions about sex? Why?

Read:

**1 Corinthians 6:18-20 , 10:13
Galatians 6:9
Romans 7:15**

    ◐ In all honesty...what would you do if you were Richard? Why?

GET A ROOM!

Kristin and Danny are sister and brother and both are in the marching band. Every Friday night they perform in the half-time show for the football game.

Normally they are required by the band director to stay for the whole game and play the team fight song after every goal. Danny, however, consumed six slices of sausage pizza during half-time and is feeling extremely ill. Kristin has a driver's license and asks Mr. Harper, the band director for permission to go home early. Seeing the green tone of Danny's complexion, Mr. Harper agrees.

Kristin and Danny walk through the front door to see their parents in the throws of passion on the living room sofa.

- If we exist on this planet, it means our parents had sex. Why is that hard to think about?

- With all the talk about teens should wait till they are married, what's wrong with mom and dad enjoying each other?

- If your parents knew you caught them—but never said anything about it, would you mention it to them or bring it up in any way later? Why?

- If you walked in on your parents and they didn't see you, what would you do? Why?

- Who do you think was more embarrassed, mom and dad or Kristin and Danny? Why?

- What should they do with the sofa now?

Read: Proverbs 5:18-19
Deuteronomy 24:5
Ephesians 5:31

- What would you do at that moment if you were Kristin or Danny? Why?

- What would you do the next day? Why?

WALLFLOWER

Martha has always felt like a wallflower—just blending right into the wallpaper, never standing out, typically ignored in social settings. She has a few close friends but has always been jealous of those people who stood out in the crowd. Those people who everyone looks up to when they enter the room.

Martha's friend Katie convinces her to dye her hair blonde to help her get noticed. So one night Martha goes to Katie's house and the two of them, using a do-it-yourself product, attempt to turn Martha's hair into "Summer Marigold" as it says on the box. The result is closer to "Carrot Top".

Martha's mother is understanding and takes her daughter to a professional the next day. The result is better but not perfect. Martha goes to school and definitely gets looked at.

She blames Katie for the fiasco and refuses to talk to her.

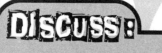

DISCUSS:

@ **Whose fault is all of this?**

@ **Should Marsha just learn to love herself as she is, or keep changing things about herself to be happier? Why?**

@ **How can we learn to be happy with who we are?**

@ **Is it good to care about what others think of us? Why?**

@ **When you screw up do you immediately try to find someone to blame it on? Why?**

@ **Should she be mad at Katie? Why?**

@ **A big complaint adults have about teenagers is "they don't take responsibility for their own actions?" Is this true?**

Read:

Galatians 6:4-5
Proverbs 17:17
Psalm 139

@ **If you were Katie what would you do? If you were Martha, what would you do? Why?**

STRIKE ONE

Jane is overwhelmed by life and has hit rock bottom-filled with profound sadness and hopelessness. She just attempted suicide. Her parents were to be away for the weekend and Jane swallowed a handful of pills from her mom's bottle of sleeping pills.

She woke up nearly 24 hours later, threw up a few times and now sits in front of the toilet wondering what to do next. There is another handful of pills in the bottle-enough to, for sure, end her life.

Her parents will be home in a few hours and her mother will eventually find the empty bottle or notice pills are missing. She doesn't have the energy to get up and move.

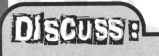

- Can you think of a time when you were overwhelmed by sadness or hopelessness? Had hit rock bottom? Talk about it.

- Do you know someone who committed or attempted suicide? Why did they do it? What other choices could they have made?

- Why do you think some people choose suicide? Explain.

- When things have been the worst in your life...what made you decide that things would get better rather than decide things would never get better-"game over"? Explain.

- What are some of the biggest reasons to live?

 **Romans 8:37-39**
Psalm 46 & 51

- In this situation, what is Jane's best course of action for the next hour? Plan it out. What should she do from here on out when she gets really down?

FAMILY TRADITION

Joann has six happily married sisters. Every girl in her family has gone to high school, gotten a two-year degree from a community college, then married and began raising children. Now that she is a senior, her family is looking at her to follow suit.

Joann has different plans. She sees no need to marry so young. She wants to go to college and major in business. She wants a corner office in a high office building. She wants to sit at the head of a table and make decisions that will affect the world. Joann has brought this up with her mother. Her mother just smiles like she knows it will never happen.

Sometimes Joann looks at her sisters, sees how happy and fulfilled they are and wonders if she's off base. She wonders if she's missing out on a bigger picture.

Discuss:

@ Is there anything wrong with the life Joann has been dreaming about that is different from that of her sisters? Explain.

@ Is our future simply our choice or should the opinions of others matter as well? Why? Who is the biggest influence on your future?

@ What would you do if your parents completely disagreed with—even adamantly opposed—your career choice (even refusing to pay for it)? Why?

Read:

Romans 12:1-2
1 Corinthians 12:4-6
Deuteronomy 30:19-20

@ If you were Joann, how would you keep the dialogue going with your parents concerning your future? Why?

WHO IS MY SISTER?

Ashley has a best friend named Jean. The two girls rarely go to Jean's house after school. On the few occasions that Ashley has been in Jean's house, she was amazed at the way Jean's parents behave. They think nothing of calling her "stupid" or poking fun at her appearance. Both girls are more comfortable studying at Ashley's house.

Last week, Jean took home a report card with two D's. The next day she came in with a swollen black eye. Ashley told her mother about it. Her mother offered Jean a place to stay if she ever needed it.

This afternoon, Jean and Ashley were studying together again. Jean showed Ashley a huge bruise on her shoulder and said, "I'd like to come and live here. Can your mother make that happen?"

Ashley called her mother at work to say that Jean will be staying with them. Her mother tells Ashley to stay in the house and lock the doors while she calls the police. Ashley didn't think her mom would call the police.

@ Would God ever want anyone to stay in a physically abusive home? Why?

@ Do you have a place you could go if things were really bad at your house? Where is that?

@ Why do so many people stay in abusive homes and other places? Explain.

@ You can't make someone leave an abusive situation but you can let them know that you will stand with them. How would you do that?

Psalm 91:9-16
Matthew 11:28
2 Corinthians 4:16-18
Ezekiel 2:6
Ecclesiastes 4:9-12

@ What would you do if you were Ashley?

@ What would you do if you were Jean?

THE FLU MEDICINE

Darlene is in the 6th grade. She is a happy girl in a middle class community. She does well in school and is active in her church.

Not long ago Darlene stayed home from school sick. Her father called his office and said that he would be working from home. That afternoon, Darlene's father gave her some flu medicine. Darlene thought it looked like an extra large dose but she took it because her father told her to. The "purple stuff" as she had called it since she was very small always had a tendency to practically knock her out. She took it and lay down to take a nap.

During her nap Darlene was sure that someone was in her room. Someone was in her bed and was touching her.

She woke up from her nap feeling sick to her stomach. Her mother is insisting she should go to a doctor tomorrow. Her father will not meet her eyes.

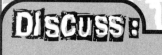

@ Is it possible to love someone who hurts you?

@ How could anyone abuse a child? Explain.

@ What should the punishment be for people who abuse children? Who abuse their own children? Why?

@ If Darlene were your best friend and told you what happened, what would you do? Why? What if you didn't believe Darlene?

**Psalm 71:1-4
2 Corinthians 4:17-18
Psalm 18:6
Numbers 11:17**

@ What would you do if you were Darlene?

MAKING ROOM OR OPENING THE DOOR?

Since her father's death, Abbey and her mother have been more like sisters than like parent and child. Abbey is now 17 and entering her senior year in high school. She remains close with her aunt (her father's sister) and uncle who live in the same town.

Recently Abbey's mother has been dating. Her mom's new boyfriend is always at the house, even when her mother is not home. He always compliments Abbey on how attractive she is. The way he looks at Abbey up and down makes her uncomfortable.

Abbey feels confident enough to mention it to her mother. To her surprise, her mother becomes angry with her and tells her she must be mistaken. A few minutes later, she sits Abbey down and tries to have a serious talk with her about how she needs to make room in her life for this new man who she loves very much. She thinks Abbey made up what she said in an attempt to keep her mom from allowing a new man to "replace" her father. Abbey is hurt that her mother doesn't believe her.

Abbey also confided in her aunt who immediately invited Abbey to come and live with them. Her mother is very upset. Abbey doesn't know what to do.

@ **Would you leave? Why?**

@ **Tell about a time when you told someone the truth about something important and they didn't believe you- or worse, thought you were lying. How do you think Abbey feels?**

@ **Have you ever known someone who had trouble adjusting to a stepparent or new family situation? What happened?**

@ **What are the issues a teenager goes through when their parent is dating someone?**

@ **Was Abbey right to share her concerns with her mother? Why do you think her mother responded as she did?**

Proverbs 3:21-24; Acts 18:10 Job 24:22-24; Malachi 4:3

@ **What are Abbey's options?**

PARTY GIRL

Friday night, Jan went to a party thrown by a girl from school. Everybody would be there. Jan drove herself and her friend Karen to the party. They met up with Nicole and the three of them had fun talking and dancing with the guys.

People snuck in a lot of alcohol. Jan held a beer in her hand but did not drink it. Karen carried around a Diet Pepsi. Nicole was drinking steadily. After a few hours, Karen told Jan she thought Nicole was drunk and that she was worried about her. Jan said that Nicole could handle it and was probably just acting wild.

An hour or so later Jan and Karen decided to leave. They found Nicole asleep in a reclining chair in the basement of the house. Several others had fallen asleep as well. Jan figured they had all told some sort of lie to their parents about where they would be. Jan drove Karen home and then went home herself.

In the morning paper Jan read that three students had been killed in a car accident while driving home from the party. Just then, the phone rang. She heard her mother talking and then crying. Her mother hung up the phone. In tears, she told Jan that it was Nicole who had driven off the road while trying to drive other teens home. Jan is devastated.

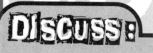

@ If there were one moment in your life you wish you could rewind and do over, what would it be? Would you do it if you could?

@ In your opinion, who is most to blame for the death of Nicole and the other teenagers? Do you think Jan shares any responsibility? Explain.

@ If Jan came to you and said she blamed herself for Nicole's death, what would you tell her? Why?

Psalm 38:4, 21-22
Micah 7:18-19
Luke 11:33-36
Proverbs 1:23, 3:5-6

@ What should Jan's next move be?

BACKSTAGE

Debbie desperately wants to try out for the spring musical in her high school. Her mother thinks she is already too busy with other things that that a lead part in a musical would be too much work. She reminds Debbie that she is not the best singer in the world, and "who are you fooling, trying out for such a role?"

Debbie decides to go for it anyway and wins the lead part. By the end of the rehearsal schedule, Debbie's grades have dropped, she has lost her place on the honor roll, she has mid-terms coming in a few weeks that she is not prepared for, and she is getting sick from the lack of sleep. Her mother's favorite phrase these days is "I told you so." But Debbie has never been happier.

Debbie's mom is continuously belittling Debbie with little insults, like "you never were the sharpest tool in the shed."

On the morning of opening night her mother greets her at breakfast with "Well, now I finally get to see what is more important than everything else in your life."

INSULTS, GRADES, PRIORITIES

- How do you keep from losing patience with someone?

- Who are the people in your life who believe in you the most? The least? Why?

- What does Debbie's passion or dream seem to be?

- What obstacles is Debbie facing? What obstacles are keeping you from finding happiness? Explain.

- What's the biggest obstacle you ever overcame? What are you still working on?

- Do you remember Joseph (the dreamer)? What happened to him as he pursued his dream?

Read: 2 Thessalonians 2:16-17
Ephesians 6:4
Matthew 25:15-20
Romans 8:17-27
Luke 21:19

- What should Debbie do? Why?

ANGER WINS

Crystal has been writing poetry for as long as she can remember. In a drawer in her room, she's saved some of the little rhymes she made up even as far back as grade school. Crystal's teacher suggested she enter some of her most recent work in a district competition. Crystal was happy to be asked and hurriedly selected three poems she thought were her best work. She never thought she'd win.

Later Crystal discovers that she won for a very personal poem she wrote when she was angry with her mother. The poem will be published in a poetry journal and she will read the poem aloud at a banquet for the winners. Crystal's mom has not yet seen or heard the winning poem. Crystal is so upset that she is seriously considering declining the award rather than expose her mother to possible public embarrassment.

@ **What would happen if Crystal withdrew from the competition?**

@ **Should she tell her mother in advance? If so, how would she phrase it? Why?**

@ **Poetry is art. Should Crystal let anything get in the way of her expressing her art—even if it might put her mother in an awkward position? Why?**

@ **How do you "work it out" when you are mad at someone? Explain.**

@ **Should Crystal have written a more politically correct, but less personal poem? Why?**

@ **What is art? Does Crystal have anything to be embarrassed about?**

@ **What might Crystal have done differently to have avoided this problem?**

1 Timothy 4:12
Colossians 3:12-14
Ephesians 4:26, 6:2, 6:4

@ **What would you do if you were Crystal?**

I AM SO PROUD OF MY KIDS!

Maria's mom looks a mess, dresses in cheap clothes, doesn't wear make-up or do her hair and is very loud. In short, she is embarrassing for Maria to be around—especially with her habit of showing even strangers every school picture ever taken of her children.

At a recent school open house, Maria was walking around trying to look like she didn't belong to the loud woman showing everyone pictures. Maria spotted her mother talking to the mother of a boy named Robert who Maria had a crush on. She knew she had to get her mother away as soon as possible. As she got closer she saw Robert join the conversation. Maria turned away; she didn't know what she would say to Robert if she got close.

As Maria was walking away, she heard her mother says, "Oh you think that's bad, you should see the haircut my daughter Maria had when she was in the fourth grade…here let me show you the picture."

DISCUSS:

@ Why does it seem parents delight in embarrassing their children?

@ Why do we care so much what others think? Explain.

@ Why would it be embarrassing for Maria's crush to see her picture?

@ When have your parents embarrassed you? How did you deal with it?

@ Do you think Maria's mom knows she embarrasses her daughter? Why?

@ Is Maria too keyed in on what others think? Explain.

@ Should Maria just love her mom the way she is? Why? Should she be angry with her mom? Why?

@ How should Maria tell her mother she was embarrassed?

@ Should Maria be angry? Why?

@ How do you deal with embarrassment? Why?

Read:

Ephesians 6:2-3
1 Peter 3:4
James 1:2-4
Ephesians 4:26, 6:2, 6:4

@ What are Maria's options?

CHAMELEON

Brad has always kept his home life and his school life separate. His parents call him Bradley while his friends call him Brad. He's mastered the art of being two different people. At home, he would never dare say a curse word.

At school Brad and his friends have made up a new catch phrase that includes profanity. (Note: If you are daring you can insert a typical phrase you may have heard from your own teens or just let it go)

To Brad and his friends it is nothing but a joke and they only use it in school. Brad and his friends were leaving school last Friday. His friend punched Brad on the arm. Brad returned the punch and repeated the catch phrase as his way of saying "Goodbye".

Brad turned and saw both his mother and father standing by the car. Apparently they had come to pick him up and take him out as a surprise.

Discuss:

@ **Have you ever felt like you try to be a different person around certain people or different crowds? Why?**

@ **Have you ever embarrassed your parents? On purpose? Talk about it.**

@ **How do you think Brad is feeling right now in front of his parents?**

@ **What would you do if you were Brad's parents? Why?**

@ **Isn't it the intent of the words that counts, not just the words? Explain.**

Read:

James 3:3-8
1 Corinthians 10:23, 13:5
Matthew 5:13-16

@ **What are Brad's choices?**

HOT INSTANT MESSAGE

Courtney and her boyfriend are very close. They've made out a few times, but have never gone beyond kissing. Courtney has always said she would wait until she was married. She's told any boyfriend she's had that they have to respect that.

Courtney has been dating Brad for a little more than a year. They often joke about having sex, but they know when to stop. Courtney was on her computer and noticed that Brad was online, so she sent him an instant message that said "I can't wait to have you rip my clothes off and let you have your way with me." The response came almost immediately. "Brad's not here right now but I'll pass along the message. Brad's dad."

@ Besides really bad timing, was there any harm in what Courtney said? Was it a sin? Explain.

@ If she and Brad have talked about sex and decided *not* to have sex, what's wrong with a joke?

@ Does it matter if Courtney and Brad are 13 or 18? Why?

@ Was Brad's father's response the right one? If you were Brad's dad would you ever mention the IM to Brad? Why?

@ Are we too hung up on what's appropriate? How so?

@ What do you think of Brad's dad's response? If you were Brad would you ever mention the sub-subject of IMs?

@ How does trust play into this story? Explain.

 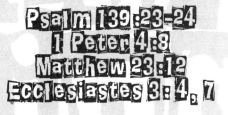

Psalm 139:23-24
1 Peter 4:8
Matthew 23:12
Ecclesiastes 3:4, 7

@ What are Courtney's options?

THAT BOY

Janice has been secretly dating an older boy. The boy is a senior and Janice is a freshman. He has been suspended once or twice. Janice has heard her mother talking about "that boy" or "that family" several times, very negatively.

Her mother would have an absolute fit if she knew that Janice wasn't always going to her friend Kelly's house but was riding around on the back of this boy's motorcycle.

Janice is completely in love. Whenever they are together he seems to drop the "tough guy" front and let her see the real him. The him that wants to go to college and major in sports medicine (though no one takes him seriously).

Unfortunately, he has an arrest record that could hurt his chances of getting into a good school. He has resigned himself to working in his dad's garage for the rest of his life.

Janice came home late last night after visiting him, telling her mother that she and Kelly had been studying late. This morning her mother told her that "that boy" from "that family" was killed last night when he drove his motorcycle into a tree and wasn't she glad now that she never went out with him.

@ How long could you keep up a solid front? Why?

@ What do you think Janice is feeling? Why?

@ In the book of Job, at first his friends grieved with him and it helped him. Should Janice say anything to anybody else? Why?

@ Would you feel guilty if you were Janice? Why?

Psalm 34:17-18
Mark 4:22
Luke 8:16
Job 2:11-13
Matthew 14:9-14

@ Should Janice say anything to her mother or should she keep it to herself forever? What would you do if you were Janice? Explain.

WHATEVER IT TAKES

Iris and her grandmother, Doris, have always been close. As Iris became a teenager, she and her grandmother became, in a lot of ways, best friends. Her grandmother listened to Iris's problems and usually offers very good advice.

Doris told Iris several times that she does not want to be kept alive by machines, or have someone use the "electric shock thingies" to bring her back if she should die. She just wants to die and be done with it.

Iris told her grandmother to write these things down or make them known to someone else. Doris always said she would, but never did.

Last week, Doris had a stroke and she is in the hospital. They have "brought her back" seven times, always at the request of Iris's mother. Her mother insists that they, "Do whatever it takes." Iris has visited her grandmother, who is unresponsive and on life support.

@ **Would you hang on to life at all costs—even if you were on life support? Why?**

@ **Would it matter if Iris were 13 or 17? Why?**

@ **Who do you think Iris's mother is most concerned with? Why?**

@ **Would you want to have someone you love hang on at all costs? Why?**

@ **Why do we fear death? Does fear of death show a lack of faith? Explain.**

@ **What are Iris' options?**

2 Corinthians 4:16-18

@ **What should Iris say to her mother? Anything else she should do? Why?**

SECURITY

Brad has been a responsible, honest kid most of his life. Since getting his driver's license, he had enjoyed the independence of going where he wants to go, usually whenever he wants. His mother also relies on him to run errands for her and to drive his little sister around.

Yesterday Zack's mother gave him a list of things to get from the grocery store. They were having company for dinner and she was out of a few things. She told Zack to hurry. In the store, Zack found what he needed and was pushing the cart out the door. A man in a suit grabbed Zack by the shoulder and held him back as he went out the door.

In the bottom of the cart was a six-pack of beer. Zack had no idea how it got there but the security guard loudly accused him of shoplifting. Zack loudly denied any wrongdoing and soon a uniformed officer was there too. Eventually Zack was able to explain everything to a manager who seemed to believe him and let him go. Zack never mentioned the event to his parents.

Zack went into the store today with is mother and little sister and was met by the security guard and told he was no longer allowed in the store.

DISCUSS:

- How many parents do you know who say, "My kid wouldn't do that" and have no idea what their kid is really like? Explain.

- Should Zack have mentioned the "problem" to his parents? Why?

- If you were the security guard would you believe Zack? Why?

- If you were Zack's parents, how would you respond when the security guard says this to your son? What would you do once you got home? Why?

Read:

Psalm 35:19-23
James 4:11
2 Thessalonians 1:5-6
Ephesians 6:2

- What is the best course of action for Zack right at this moment?

@ Think of life as a swimming pool. What are the weights in your life? What are the things that keep your head above water?

@ When was the last time you thought you had hit bottom? Did you stay there? Why?

@ Why do you think teenagers commit suicide?

@ If a suicidal friend asked you for one good reason they should choose to live, what would you tell him or her?

John 16:33
1 Peter 5:7
John 10:27-29
Galatians 6:9

@ What should Trish do to be sure she never hits bottom again? Explain.

TAKE NOTES/MAKE NOTES

EMBARRASSED

Jenna is sure that Robert is the cutest boy in the whole world. He used to be a geek and a jerk. When he would come over to her house to hang out with her brother, they would be so obnoxious that she couldn't stand to be in the same room with them.

Now Robert is 17 and handsome. Jenna has flirted with him and he has flirted back. They have a tendency to stare at each other for long periods of time, until her brother can't stand to be in the same room with them. She keeps hoping that Robert will ask her to the homecoming dance next month, but so far he hasn't mentioned it.

Yesterday, Jenna thought she was alone in the house and came out of the shower to find she had no clean blue jeans. Believing she was alone, she wrapped a towel around herself and ran as fast as she could to the laundry room to get some clothes. She turned the corner and collided head-on into her brother and Robert.

Down they all went...along with her towel. She fell to the floor and screamed, trying desperately to cover herself, then ran to her bedroom. She didn't come out until the next morning.

Jenna's mother told her she just needs to keep her head high and laugh about it. She knows her father has threatened her brother with some sort of punishment if he doesn't keep his mouth shut, because he keeps laughing at her and teasing.

Monday morning she goes to school and Robert won't even look at her. She's convinced that he thinks she's ugly and will never ask her out.

TAKE NOTES/MAKE NOTES

DISCUSS:

@ When has something embarrassing like this happened to you?

@ What's the most embarrassing thing that ever happened to you?

@ Has anyone ever been super-embarrassed in front of you?

@ What happened? What did you do?

@ What's the worst that could happen to Jenna at this point?

@ Why do you think Robert won't look at her?

@ Should Jenna make the first move and talk to Robert? Why?

@ If you were Jenna's best friend, what advice would you offer?

@ If you were Robert's best friend, what advice would you offer?

Read:
1 Corinthians 13:4-7
Colossians 3:12-15

@ If you were Jenna, what would you do?

TAKE NOTES/MAKE NOTES

INVITED

Myrna can't stand the idea of missing her last homecoming dance. She and her boyfriend broke up two weeks ago. She already has a dress and bought the tickets.

Most of the guys she really wants to go out with already have dates. Those guys that don't have dates are the guys she doesn't want to go out with anyway. Her best friend Nancy has invited her to join her and her boyfriend, but Myrna doesn't want to be a third wheel.

Four days before the dance, a boy named Walter called her and managed an invitation between his nervous stutters and stammers. Walter is not exactly the homecoming king type she was hoping would ask her to go. He isn't very popular and, though attractive, is painfully shy. She told Walter that she would think about it and let him know.

@ **What's wrong with going out just for fun? Does dating have to be so serious? Must it always be an "image" thing? Explain.**

@ **Is Myrna being selfish? Explain.**

@ **Have you ever gone out with someone just because they would look good "on your arm"? Just to get to go to a particular party? Is this okay? Why?**

@ **Should Myrna go to the dance with Walter?**

Philippians 2:3-4
Luke 6:31

@ **What should Myrna do?**

@ **What would you do if you were Walter?**

CALLING HOME

John has a weakness for following people when they do stupid things. He even knows that he's doing something stupid at the time, but he seems to go right along every time.

He has gone on a weekend retreat with his youth group and dozens of other youth groups from all around the district. John's youth director has said that rules will be followed and there will be no messing around-or parents will have to drive the 3 hours to pick up their misbehaving child.

John met two guys during the day and they shot hoops for a few hours. The two guys said they were going to sneak out in the middle of the night and walk a quarter mile through the woods. The path lets out near the highway and they're going to go to a convenience store. They're not drinking or smoking, they just feel like sneaking out. John agrees to go with them.

They arrive at the store and one of the guys tries to buy a six-pack. In the store is an undercover county sheriff who "escorts" them back to the camp. The youth directors are awakened and John finds himself sitting by a phone where his youth minister has told him to call and ask his mother to come and get him.

@ **When there are lots of kids on a retreat, why are leaders so strict on the rules?**

@ **Okay, they made a mistake-it wasn't like the guys killed somebody or stole from the store-so is there really anything to get upset about? Explain.**

@ **What would be your first words when mom or dad picks up the phone? Why? What would your parents do?**

@ **Would you rather make the phone call, or try and talk your way out of it? Why?**

 **1 Thessalonians 5:12-13
Hebrews 13:17**

@ **How should John handle the call with his parents? How should he resolve the issue with the leaders? Why?**

ALL PRAYERS

Last week, Barry's grandfather had a heart attack. The paramedics "brought him back" and he has been close to dying four times since then. Each time, the family shows up and Barry's mother begins to weep. But somehow, his grandfather always seems to come back from the edge. Sometimes his eyes are open and he seems coherent.

Barry looked at the frail bag of bones in the bed and barely recognized his grandfather. Barry excused himself from the room and found the hospital chapel. Alone in the small room he knelt down and prayed.

"God if you are really up there and you really love my grandfather then take him now and stop letting him suffer. Amen." By the time Barry got back to the room on the fourth floor his grandfather was gone. Barry's mother was sobbing so uncontrollably that she had to be sedated. His father is crying as well. The nurse had to go over and close his grandfather's eyes.

@ **Some people say, "Be careful what you pray for—you just might get it." What does that mean? Explain.**

@ **Do you think the timing here was coincidence? Why?**

@ **Would you tell someone what you prayed if you were Barry?**

@ **Was Barry's prayer a selfish or selfless one? Explain.**

@ **Does God answer all prayers?**

1 Peter 4:12-13
2 Corinthians 5:1-8
Romans 5:3-5

@ **Should Barry feel guilty? If not, how should he feel? Why?**

UNWELCOME

Kevin walked the block to the school. It was easily three times the size of his old school and the volume of the students hanging around outside could be heard before he got to the parking lot. He navigated carefully through a huge crowd of kids just outside the door and walked into the school.

Immediately after walking inside, he felt a hand on his shoulder. He turned and found himself looking up into the face of a big black kid who seemed to tower over him.

"You lost?" The kid asked.

"No, I'm just new here," Kevin said.

The kid didn't smile. "Let me fill you in. This is our entrance. You don't use this entrance. White boys and girls can use the entrance on the other side."

Kevin looked around. He was the only white person he could see. His last school had only white students and Kevin has no idea what to do or why this guy seems to hate him.

- When have you experienced racism? When have you had a racist attitude or done something racist?

  - How prevalent is racism in your school? Bullying? Explain.

- Does anybody hate you?

- Where does bigotry come from?

  - What do you think feeds racism and causes people to hate just based on skin color?

    - Would you simply pass by and walk to your class or leave the school and walk in the other entrance for white people?

Acts 10:34-35
Colossians 3:7-10

- How should Kevin respond? Why?

SHOT

Greg's head was pounding as loud as his heart. He wiped sweat out of his eyes with the edge of his soaking uniform. The score was tied. There were three seconds left. He had one foul shot. His stomach was in his throat. His buddy Tom nodded at him from the left side, saying "You can do this!" He turned and saw Mitch on the other side

Mitch hated his guts. Every time he makes a shot, Mitch called it lucky. Every time he misses a shot, Mitch rants and raves at him. Mitch's eyes said, "Don't screw this up, you moron." Greg turned back to Tom who mouthed the words "Do it!"

Greg bounced the ball two times. He felt the sweat between his fingers and the ball.

He felt the sweat between his fingers and the ball. He pushed the ball up and watched as it sailed high over the backboard and came straight down nearly hitting a trumpet player who played with the pep band. Within a moment the game was over.

@ **Talk about a time when you pinned your hopes on something and lost.**

@ **Explain how a team functions when it is functioning at its best. How is Greg's team functioning?**

@ **Do you perform better under pressure or worse? Why?**

@ **Would you say you are more discouraged by others or more encouraged? Explain.**

@ **When have you felt like you let "everybody" down? Explain.**

@ **If you were Greg's coach what would you say to him at the next practice? What would you say to the team?**

@ **Is it fair to say that Greg lost the game?**

@ **How do you support your friends?**

Ephesians 4:15-16
Psalm 34:18

@ **What question do you have for Greg?**

PERFECT TO IMPERFECT

Susan had been hoping Kyle would ask her out for the past half year. He finally did. It was just McDonald's and a movie but it was a great Saturday afternoon, first date.

They saw a great "date flick," not romantic, but not "blood and gore." They both laughed and when the popcorn was gone, he held her hand. Holding his hand was "electric" and she had a really good feeling. Later at McDonald's, they ordered. He paid and they sat in the back.

They began to eat and Kyle took a huge bite of his sandwich and immediately began to speak with his mouth full. "Whad oo tink of mofie?"

She looked at him. "What?"

He said it again. This time, a bit of food shot out of his mouth and hit her cheek. He smiled, wiped her cheek and kept on chomping loudly, still not closing his mouth. She kept trying not to look at him, but when she didn't look, all she could hear was his loud chomping and somehow that seemed even more disgusting. She had never been so disgusted at watching another person eat. Suddenly, there was no part of her that wanted to go out with this guy ever again.

DISCUSS:

@ What happened here? Explain.

@ Is this one of those little things that could be ignored? Is it reason to never date someone again?

@ What are some "things" that just get under your skin when you are talking with someone? Why?

@ How could Susan's feelings change so quickly?

@ What are some little things that are immediate turn-off's for you? Explain.

@ What sort of expectations do girls put on a date?

@ What sort of expectations do guys put on a date?

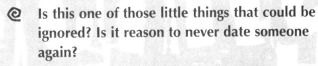

Read: Luke 6:41-42
2 Timothy 1:7
Proverbs 4:23

@ If you were Susan would you go out with Kyle again? Why?

ADULT EDUCATION

Terry needed some extra help in geometry—his grades were slipping. He asked his teacher, Mr. Collins about it and Mr. Collins said to come by anytime there was no class and he would be glad to help. Two days later, Terry finished his lunch early and went to Mr. Collin's classroom.

Terry peeked into the room and saw there was no class. He couldn't see Mr. Collins' desk from the window so he opened the door and went in. He caught the last moment of a passionate kiss between Mr. Collins and Mrs. Stine. When they noticed Terry, they immediately began acting like nothing had happened.

Mrs. Stine grabbed a stack of papers off his desk and said, "Okay then, I'll look these over and I'll get back to you on that other thing." She said "Hi" to Terry on her way out and Mr. Collins said "Okay, let's take a look at what problems you're having." Terry is still in shock.

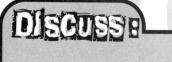

@ Have you ever walked in at the wrong moment? Talk about it.

    @ If you were in Terry's place, would you say anything to anybody? What would you say and to who?

@ Would it make a difference if either or both of the teachers were married to other people? Why?

    @ How might Terry's respect for these teachers change after this? Why?

@ If this is an affair, is it a simple mistake or a bigger problem? Why?

    @ What should Mr. Collins say to Terry?

    @ What should Terry say to Mr. Collins or Ms. Stine?

Proverbs 11:12
James 3:5-6

@ What should Terry do?

LESSONS LEARNED

Douglas is 15. For years he's watched his father mow their lawn and come in from outside, throw his shirt in the laundry room and open a cold beer.

Douglas picked up the lawn mowing duties last year. Both his parents are out of the house and Douglas was told to have the lawn mowed before they got home. Douglas finished in plenty of time and walked into the house, dripping with sweat. He thought for only a moment about what to do. He tossed his sweaty t-shirt into the laundry and opened a cold beer. Sitting down in the chair his father always sat in, he finished the beer.

Douglas wasn't sure if he liked the taste or not. He just knew he liked the idea that he was drinking a cold beer after mowing the lawn. He felt grown up. He put the bottle at the bottom of the garbage can and covered it carefully with trash. Since he also was the one who took the garbage to the curb, he doubted it would be found. He took a shower and got dressed. He brushed his teeth to cover up any beer breath and went out into the kitchen. His father was there, loading the dishwasher.

"Lawn looks good, thanks," his father said.

"You're welcome," Douglas said and went to the refrigerator.

"You want to tell me what this is?" Douglas' dad said as he tossed a beer bottle top at him. Douglas caught it.

DISCUSS:

⦿ **What activities do you do you do that make you seem most "mature"? What activities make you feel grown up? Why?**

⦿ **What did Doug do that showed he was immature? Mature?**

⦿ **What drives us, when young, to appear older?**

⦿ **What do you think of Doug's beer drinking?**

⦿ **Was Doug's dad a bad example or was Doug just being stupid? Explain.**

⦿ **What should Doug's first response be?**

Read:

Ephesians 6:1-4
1 Corinthians 10:23

⦿ **You are Doug...your Dad just asked the question...ready...go.**

PARTY PLANS

Dave and Henry have been friends for years. When Dave's parents said they were going out of town for the weekend, Dave and Henry both thought the same thing—"party!" Preparations began before Dave's parents were even gone. As they left, Dave's parents sternly warned him, "No parties!"

Henry would stay over and help Dave get everything cleaned up before his parents got back, late Sunday afternoon. The party was wild and crazy. Some of their friends brought alcohol.

Two guys got in an argument over a girl and someone was pushed down (turning over a table), but ultimately there was no damage to the house. Both Dave and Henry thought it went great.

Sunday morning the two of them cleaned the house from top to bottom. Sunday afternoon, Dave and Henry were playing video games. When his parents got home, his mother came through the door and said, "How was the party?" Dave and Henry were stunned and said nothing.

"The house looks pretty good," she said, "but there's a puddle of vomit on my front porch and what looks like a bowling alley of beer bottles on the driveway.

@ When was the last time you got caught hiding something from your parents? What happened?

@ Nobody got hurt and the house looks clean, so what's the problem with what Henry and Dave did? Explain.

@ Could Dave and Henry plead ignorance to the evidence? Why?

@ If a tree falls in the forest and no one is there to hear it, does it make a sound?

@ If trust is broken and the person who broke it got away with it completely…does it matter? Why?

Read:

1 Corinthians 13:11
1 Peter 4:7-8
Proverbs 28:13

@ What should Dave and Henry do?

CUSTOMER SATISFACTION

Doug and his friends went to Chubby Charlie's for dinner. Chubby's is a bar-b-q restaurant that serves really good food.

Charlie noticed a guy from his gym class was working there as a waiter. This was a guy who repeatedly hit Doug when the coach wasn't looking and who enjoyed throwing the soccer ball at Doug's crotch. The guy barely looked at Charlie as he and his friends placed an order.

Sitting on the table were the Customer Comment Cards. Doug picked one up and wrote several nasty untrue (but believable) things about the waiter and the service. A few days later Doug overheard the same kid in his gym class talking about how he got fired from his job as a waiter and he didn't know why.

@ Is this a case of the bully getting what he deserved? Why?

@ What if the guy was a trustworthy and reliable worker at the restaurant, would that change anything? Why?

@ If this guy was supporting his family, would that change anything? Why?

@ Is forgiveness always the right thing to do and taking revenge always the wrong thing to do? Why?

@ What's the most you've ever forgiven someone? Why?

@ How long should you "take it" before you shouldn't have to anymore? Explain.

@ How else could Doug have handled this situation?

John 8:7
2 Corinthians 9:10

@ What would you do if you were Doug?

TAKE NOTES/MAKE NOTES

ONLY CONSTANT IN LIFE—CHANGE

Hanover's Bakery has been a major part of Maggie's life for as long as she can remember. Whenever her mother needs to donate something to a school bake sale, it usually winds up coming from Hanover's.

Mr. and Mrs. Hanover have been running the bakery for more than fifty years. Mr. Hanover bakes and Mrs. Hanover is the cashier. There's always a college student in the back scrubbing pans.

One of Maggie's fondest memories is when her father woke her up early one Sunday morning and asked if she wanted to go to Hanover's with him.

Mrs. Hanover always gave a free cookie for every "A" on a report card. To Maggie, Hanover's Bakery is one of the best places in the world.

Maggie stopped by Hanover's last weekend on her way to softball practice to see a sign that said "New Owners." She went in and didn't recognize the woman behind the counter.

"Where's Mrs. Hanover?" She asked.

"They retired," the surly woman said, "What do you want?"

Maggie ordered one of her favorite blueberry muffins to go but she knew as soon as she bit into it that it wasn't the same as what Mr. Hanover made. She threw the rest of it away and drove on to school.

What is Maggie going through right now? Why?

What are some things in your life of which you have fond memories…but that have now changed? Explain.

As teenagers we want things to change quickly but at the same time we want some things to always stay the same. What are some things in your life you hope to see changed soon? What are some things in your life that you hope will never change? Why?

@ What's the biggest change you've ever gone through? Explain.

@ Would you rather change things on your own or have them changed by outside forces? Would you rather see it coming or be surprised? Would you rather have things change in little increments or have it happen all at once? Why?

@ How well do you accept things that you can't change? Why?

 **Read:** **Philippians 3:15-16 2 Corinthians 12:4-12**

@ How should Maggie respond to all this?

TAKE NOTES/MAKE NOTES

DRESSING UP

Michelle likes bright-colored socks. No matter what sort of fashion trend is going on, she's always worn a pair of bright-colored socks with just about every outfit. She has all colors in day-glo bright.

The only time she quit wearing them was during her freshman year, when some now-forgotten pop star started wearing them. Back then, every girl in her school started wearing them. Once the pop star was off the charts and the girls in her school stopped wearing the socks, Michelle started wearing them again.

Michelle's boyfriend asked her to the senior prom and jokingly asked her if she was going to wear socks to match her formal gown. It is an idea she has not been able to get out of her head. She's always been known for wearing them so why not? Her mother is mortified at the idea. She says that 25 years from now she'll look back at the yearbook and regret wearing the socks.

Michelle thinks people will look at their yearbooks and remember who she was. Michelle's friends say she's crazy. Her boyfriend refuses to have an opinion at all. Her gown for the prom is white with a tremendous amount of lace.

Michelle found a bright pair of orange, green, striped socks. She keeps looking at the socks and wondering if they will go with the new pair of high-heeled shoes her mother found to go with the dress.

TAKE NOTES/MAKE NOTES

DISCUSS:

@ Do you think Michelle will look back with embarrassment on the bright socks she is wearing now? Why?

@ Would you go out with Michelle? ("Mike", if you're a girl)

@ Do teenagers have a bad sense of the future? Explain.

@ Have you ever looked at your parent's high school yearbook with them? What do they say? Do they share any regrets? Explain.

@ What is your trademark? How do you want to be remembered in your high school?

@ If you could chose, your secret wish for your being named "most likely to..." would be what?

Read:

Psalm 139:14-17
Romans 12:2

@ If you were Michelle, how would you try and sell your decision to your mother? Why?

TAKE NOTES/MAKE NOTES

THE VIEW FROM HERE

Charlotte is a 9th grader who plays flute in the marching band. The band goes to all the "away" games, riding school buses. Charlotte and her best friend, Annette, were early and got one of the coveted back seats.

After the game, the busses are heading home in the dark. In the seat in front of Charlotte and Annette sit one of the flag girls and a drummer. The bus begins to move and these two immediately begin to give each other dental exams with their tongues and begin groping one another. Charlotte and Annette look at each other wondering if the couple will ever stop, but the scene gets even more intense.

The flag-girl opens her eyes and catches Charlotte staring disapprovingly.

"Take a picture, it'll last longer," she says, resuming the tongue exam of her boyfriend's mouth—and the groping.

"Get a room!" Charlotte says, but the couple ignores her.

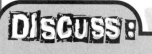

- What's a good comeback line Charlotte could have used?

- What is your personal opinion about PDAs (public displays of affection)? Best left in private? Explain.

- Is it any of Charlotte's business what the couple does in their seat? Why?

- If someone is smoking near you, would you ask them to put it out or would you just move your seat? Why?

- How do you handle rude or obnoxious behavior of others? Why?

Psalm 39:1-3
Proverbs 11:12

- What would you do if you were Charlotte?

INTRUSION

Dave is one of six students in the advanced art class in his high school. He really feels this is what he was meant to do with his life. His teacher feels he has real talent and has offered to write letters of recommendation for him to several art schools in other states.

Most of the class in advanced art is individual study. Each student gets to create an original piece of art, whether a sculpture, a painting, or whatever. Dave likes to paint and has put his heart into a piece he has titled *Intrusion*. Dave's religious beliefs have led him to believe that war, under any circumstance, is wrong and that there are always other ways of settling conflict.

The United States is currently fighting alongside another nation that is trying to remain independent. Dave feels that this is not a war the US should be fighting. His senior project reflects this. His is not a popular opinion.

Dave's art teacher has encouraged his passion and told him to go for it and enter his piece in the county art show where he could win a scholarship. The principal has decided that Dave's work does not represent the school well and will not allow it to be displayed in the senior art show. He will also not give Dave his endorsement for the district art contest.

@ Which is more important, an art contest and possible scholarship or Dave's convictions? Why?

@ What would you do if you were Dave's teacher?

@ When have you found yourself on the opposite side of popular opinion? How did that feel?

@ It's just one painting and the scholarship affects the rest of his life...why shouldn't Dave just submit another piece?

Ecclesiastes 3:7
Matthew 10:38-39

@ What would you do if you were Dave?

DOWN TO SIZE

Joe's older sister is constantly putting him down. All his life, he recalls her taking things from him and telling him what to do. "What's mine is mine and what's yours is mine," he remembers hearing from her once when they were children.

Whatever he does, she tries to do it one better. Whatever happens in school, she feels compelled to tell him she already did that and why she is better at it than he is.

Joe has discovered a passion for history. He makes straight A's and his teacher invited him to be in a History competition that only a few students get invited to this year. History is something that his sister cannot stand.

Joe realizes part of his love of the subject comes from the fact that he finally has something that will be just his, that is sister can't take from him. She keeps telling him that only geeks go out for these competitions and that he will probably just choke under the pressure, embarrassing the family. It is the morning of the competition and Joe's mom is arguing with his sister, telling her she has to go and support her brother.

- ☺ What's Joe's sister's problem? Explain.

- ☺ Should Joe's sister have to go? Why?

- ☺ Does Joe's sister love him? Explain.

- ☺ Why do some people have to be in control over their siblings? Do you know anyone like that?

- ☺ Do you know someone with an if-I-can't-have-it-you-can't-have-it attitude? How do you deal with that person?

- ☺ Is it easy or hard for you to see someone close to you do well? Why?

Galatians 6:2-6
Hebrews 12:14-16

- ☺ What would you do if you were Joe?

FOUR-TIME FAILURE

Charlie is 16 and is taking his driver's test for the fourth time. The first time he made a stupid mistake and knows that he deserved to fail. The second and third time he drew Officer Rocker as his examiner. Officer Rocker has been there for twenty years.

Two of Charlie's teachers remember taking their test with Officer Rocker and failing. No one that Charlie has talked to that took the driver's test with Officer Rocker passed it the first time. But Charlie has now drawn him twice and has failed both times.

Charlie's friends all seem to have their licenses. They're making comments about why he doesn't have his. His mother has told him that if he doesn't pass this time she won't be driving him back to the license bureau anymore. If he doesn't pass this time, his permit will expire and he will have to take the written test all over again as well.

DISCUSS:

@ **How important is a driver's license to a teenager? Why?**

@ **Have you ever met someone who seemed to appoint himself or herself as a "gate keeper", controlling access to cool things or privileges? Why?**

@ **How would you feel if you failed the driver's test four times? Why?**

@ **Is it possible Charlie has just found an excuse? Do you know people who always seem to have one? Why is it important to avoid looking for an excuse for failures or mistakes?**

@ **How many times will you try something to get what you want? Why?**

@ **Tell about the last person that made you feel stupid. Did you deserve it? Why?**

@ **How might this challenge help shape Charlie's character? Explain.**

@ **Talk about the last person to give you a (mental or physical) dope slap? Did you deserve it?**

Read:

Romans 5:3-5
Proverbs 15:22

@ **What should Charlie do to make sure he passes the driving test next time? Explain.**

MEMORY LOSS

The last thing that Ray remembers is looking at his shoes. He's not sure why this sticks in his mind. He now lies in a hospital room. His mother and father are there and a police officer is trying to ask him questions. His head hurts.

He sees the bandages on his hand and he has no memory of how he got here. He remembers being invited to the party. He remembers telling his parents he was going to a movie with a few friends. He remembers the pretty girl from another school at the party. He remembers looking at his shoes.

The police officer is named Tanya. She talks quietly when she talks to him but he can see how agitated his parents are behind her.

Officer Tanya said that someone slipped a drug into the drinks of several of the students at the party. Ray apparently got some of this. She says that he got into a car with some others. They have what they think is Ray's best friend Gibbs, but they can't identify him. There were three others in the car and two of them are dead.

One girl is in a coma. Her name is Molly. Ray thinks that's the name of the girl from the other school, but he doesn't remember. He doesn't remember anything.

 **DISCUSS:**

@ How do you think Ray feels right now? Why?

@ In this situation would you want to remember?

@ Should Ray's parents punish him for lying and sneaking out? Why?

@ How responsible is Ray for all that's happened? After all, he lied to his parents and went to the party. Does he share any of the blame? Why?

@ Why do tragedies happen? Is it dumb luck, coincidence, or God's plan? Explain.

@ Who do you talk to when things get real bad?

@ How does God view and respond to such tragedies? Explain.

@ Does God cry?

 **Read:**

Romans 8:28-29
Ephesians 1:11

@ What should Ray do to get some peace? To overcome the pain? To grieve? To find forgiveness? Why?

OVER-DEVELOPED?

Kim has come to hate her body. She never wanted to look the way she does, but it isn't her fault. She started to "develop" when she was 10. At 16, her breasts are big, bigger than her mother's—and any other girl's she knows. They are bigger than any models she has seen in a magazine.

She can't stand the way guys and even older men look at her. Most of them don't even care if she notices—like she is nothing more than breasts, not even a person. They probably think she must like the attention. Even a few of her teachers stare at her chest when they talk to her. When she complains to her friends, they are disbelieving, "Yeah, right, I am sure you've got it tough!"

Kim drove by the local college last week, and at a stop light, a car full of college guys yelled things out the window that brought her to tears. Kim finally told her mother that her size made her miserable. Her mother is sympathetic, but doesn't understand how deeply Kim feels about it. Kim asked her doctor about plastic surgery to have her breasts reduced. She will need a parent's okay.

@ **If you could change one thing about yourself physically, what would it be? Explain.**

@ **Why is it easy to believe the "beautiful people" or people with a "bod" have fewer problems than others do?**

@ **Is Kim being selfish? Why?**

@ **Why is it difficult to see past the "now" and look at the possibilities of the future?**

@ **Do most people believe that those with good bodies adhere to the credo "if you've got it, flaunt it"? Explain.**

@ **Should we ever change how God made us? What is the upside of such changes (benefits)? The downside (risks)?**

**Ephesians 2:20-24
Jeremiah 29:11**

@ **If you were Kim, what would you do?**

THE RIGHT TO VOTE

Sam's parents have long supported a string of politically conservative candidates for the senate position from their district. This year, the mayor of their town is running for the senate position that opened when the current senator was caught having an affair with his secretary. Both of Sam's parents campaigned for the out-going senator.

Sam's mother was one of the ones in charge of the mayor's last campaign. His mother and father are consumed with the campaign. Sam will be eligible to vote by the time the election rolls around and his father has already offered to drive him to register to vote the day after his eighteenth birthday.

The problem is that Sam does not want to endorse his parents' candidate. He remembers stuffing envelopes for their candidate as a kid. He remembers the first time he started reading the mailers and figuring out that he didn't agree with what the candidate stood for on key issues that would affect Sam and his generation.

DISCUSS:

@ How long until you can vote? Will you vote at your first available opportunity? Why?

@ What issues today do you feel most strongly about?

@ What's an issue that would make you vote, or not vote, for a particular candidate?

@ If your parents are both Democrats does that mean you have to be? Why?

@ Do you feel pressure from your parents to vote as a Republican, Democrat, or independent? Why?

@ Should Sam disclose to his parents how he intends to vote, or just keep it to himself? Why?

@ What's the biggest choice you think you will ever make?

Read:

James 1:19
Romans 13:1

@ What would you do if you were Sam?

126

LISTEN UP!

Barbara's parents have gone to yet another of those seminars on "How to Communicate With Your Teenager." Barbara hates it when they go to those kind of things. They always share details about her that she doesn't want shared. And they always wind up making friends with another couple who come over for coffee afterward. When her parents get home with their new friends in tow, she just knows her parents are saying, "See, this is the girl we told you about. Now watch her and see if we aren't right."

Barbara doesn't see a lot of problem with the current state of her relationship with her parents. Her grades are mostly good. She stays out of trouble. She considers herself an average teenager, but her parents seem to see everything she does as a "warning sign" of future problems. They keep sitting her down and having "adult" conversations. She's sick of it and lately has been wondering if she ought to give them something to worry about.

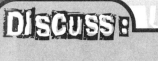

@ Have you ever done something because you know it would tick off your parents? Teacher? Sibling? Boss? Explain.

@ Why do you think that once parents have seen you in diapers, they have trouble seeing you as an adult?

@ Do your parents try too hard in their relationship with you, or do they not try hard enough? Explain.

@ Barbara's parents are trying to do what they can to be good parents, so why do you think Barbara views what they are doing as a problem for her? Explain.

@ Besides "giving her parents something to worry about", what are some other approaches Barbara can use to communicate her feelings to her parents? Explain.

@ What's the best way to prove we can be spoken to as an adult?

@ Who is easier for you to talk to about "that kind of stuff"...mom or dad? Why do you suppose that is?

@ Are Barb's parents doing anything wrong?

Psalm 143:10
Proverbs 11:14

@ What should Barb do?

THIS FAR

Kent is quite proud of himself for the way he's made it through the last two years—ever since his parents divorced. He and his mother both work to make ends meet. He's seen his father a few times and talks on the phone with him once every few months, but he lives on the other side of the United States now.

Kent's dad cheated on his mother and when the lawyers came in, the divorce got very ugly. Both his parents were called into the judge's chambers and told to back off each other and settle things. Kent has listened to both parents bad mouth the other. There were times that he wasn't sure that he would live through this at all. Now he has and he's feeling pretty good about himself.

Kent's dad has married the woman with whom he had the affair. They've asked Kent to spend the summer with them. Kent still carries some anger toward his new stepmother for breaking up his parents' marriage, but has accepted that they are married now—no turning back.

Kent's mother won't let him go to the other side of the country. Kent's dad said that he would pay for the plane ticket. They spent a lot of time arguing about it on the phone. Neither one has asked Kent what he wants.

Just listening to his mother yell on the phone is starting to bring back some of the bad feelings he hasn't felt in months.

TAKE NOTES/MAKE NOTES

DISCUSS:

@ Divorce hurts, more than death sometimes because the pain keeps coming. How long does it take to forgive someone who hurt you?

@ If divorce is a deep well and the children are stuck at the bottom, what would you say "the rope" is? Who is usually there to help them out?

@ Two years have elapsed, so should Ken's anger be resolved toward his stepmother? Why?

@ Have you ever tried to tell someone who was angry not to be angry? How'd that go?

@ Should Kent step in and say what he'd like to do this summer (and risk seeming to favor one parent over another), or just let his parents fight it out and stay out of it? Why?

@ How can a person get out from between two arguing people and still be there to offer support?

Read: Psalm 27:4-5
Matthew 7:24-27

@ What would you do if you were Kent? Why?

TAKE NOTES/MAKE NOTES

MORE THAN CLOSE?

Sophia and Denise first met in kindergarten. They were playing hopscotch on the playground when a ball the boys were playing with came flying over and hit Sophia in the back. Denise kicked the ball over the fence and the boys got in trouble. Sophia and Denise have been friends ever since.

The girls are both 16 now. They have supported each other through it all. Sophia was there when Denise's dad had cancer. Denise was there for Sophia when her brother was killed overseas in an army training accident. They've been there for each other when the guys they liked didn't like them, through bad grades, through attacks from jealous girls and all the drama of life. When they were 14 they even promised each other that if they ever fell for the same guy that they would both stop liking him in order to save the friendship—they were very close.

Denise has noticed lately that Sophia has been a lot more attentive. She touches and hugs more than she used to. She is being "flirty." She likes to brush Denise's hair like she did when they were kids, but really makes a big deal about how much she loves her hair and how beautiful Denise is.

Denise thinks that Sophia s coming onto her with some kind of sexual motivation. Sophia wants to take their friendship in another direction. She has become very uncomfortable. she doesn't even know how, or whether, to share her discomfort with Sophia.

TAKE NOTES/MAKE NOTES

DISCUSS:

@ Would you rather find out your best friend was a murderer or gay? Why?

@ How difficult would it be for you if your best friend suddenly turned out to be gay? Why?

@ Think for a moment about the deepest secret you've ever confided in someone. What would you do if he or she told someone else? Why?

@ What would you do if you found out your best friend was gay and everyone thought you were to by association? Why?

@ Is Sophia overreacting or does she have enough evidence to go on? Explain.

@ How difficult a topic would this to be to discuss with your best friend? Why?

@ If your best friend was gay, how tough would it be for you if everyone thought you were gay by association? Why?

Read:

Proverbs 15:29
Philippians 4:8

@ What would you do if you were Denise?

TAKE NOTES/MAKE NOTES

FRIENDSHIP, HOMOSEXUALITY, COMMUNICATION

LEARNING LESSONS

Derek and his family have long made jokes about the way his mother drives. When Derek was still small and in the backseat he once said that, "When Mommy drives the yellow light means go very fast." It has been a family joke ever since.

Derek is 15 and will be getting his driver's permit soon. On the way to the grocery store, Derek's mother burns the yellow light and for the first time that Derek can remember, she gets pulled over. Derek's mother begins a long detailed lie to the police officer. His mother doesn't get the ticket. His mom smiles and waves to the officer as they pull away.

Immediately she gets angry and starts complaining about cops with "nothing better to do." Derek wants to point out that she was the one who ran the yellow light (and a little of the red). He also wants to remind her of the long lecture on honest and integrity he received last week when he said he was studying at a friend's house but instead was at the mall.

℗ In one sentence, define integrity.

℗ Should Derek just keep his mouth shut or should he take this opportunity to confront his mother over her lapse in integrity? Why?

℗ Is there anything wrong with the kind of lie Derek's mother told? Explain.

℗ Is it ever okay to not be honest? Explain.

Proverbs 11:3
Ephesians 4:25

℗ If you were Derek and you wanted to bring your mom's integrity lapse up to her…when and how would you do it?

LEFT ALONE

Gary's father died three days ago. His father was a fireman who had a heart attack while pulling some people out of a burning building. The papers have called him a hero.

A few hours ago they "laid him to rest"—a phrase which Gary hates. He is so sick of sympathy and pity that he wants to scream. If one more person puts a hand on his shoulder and says something kind, he may explode. He has tried several times to escape to his room, but his mother always calls him back.

People are trying to "be strong" around him and not show a lot of emotion. At the same time, they keep wondering why Gary hasn't cried. He wishes they would figure out what they want. Do they want him to be strong or do they want him to cry?

He doesn't want to meet more of his father's co-workers. He doesn't want to hear the minister come up with Bible sayings that are supposed to make him feel better. He wants to be left alone. But most of all, he wants things to go back to the way they were just four days ago.

@ **What is Gary going through? Why does he seem angry? Explain.**

@ **What advice would you offer Gary?**

@ **What happens when all you want is something that isn't possible? How do you get over that?**

@ **How long does it take to get tired of pity?**

@ **What good does it do to be angry? Explain.**

@ **Have you ever been angry with God? Why? What happened?**

**Psalm 42:6-11
Matthew 14:13-14**

@ **If you were Gary, what would you do next?**

BEST-LAID PLANS

Fran can't stand to be in her own home anymore. Her mother has run her life from the time she was an infant. Her mother has chosen her friends, picked out her clothes, planned her free time, and sent her to enough Bible Summer Camps to make Fran know the Scriptures inside and out. To her, the Bible has become just words, just something to memorize.

Fran's mother has tried to set Fran up with the sons of her friends from church. Every time Fran goes out with a boy, her mother starts asking questions about him, wondering how good a son-in-law he would be. Fran's mother has chosen several colleges for Fran to pick from.

Fran can't remember the last time her mother asked if she was happy. Fran has decided that she has to do something to throw a wrench into her mother's plans. She thinks that maybe if she was pregnant, her mother would throw her out of the house and she could finally be free. She dismisses this idea as stupid, but it keeps coming back to her mind.

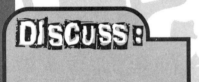

@ What was the last important decision you made entirely on your own?

@ What was the last important decision you made that turned out to be entirely the wrong one?

@ Has Fran's mother had too much control in her life? Explain.

@ Who has the most influence in your life?

@ Why would Fran consider resorting to such extreme measures as becoming pregnant? Explain.

@ Will getting pregnant solve any of Fran's problems? Explain.

Romans 12:12
Hebrews 5:14
Luke 14:16-19

@ If Fran mentioned this to you at the lunch table, what would you say to her?

CHRISTMAS COMPLAINTS

Jason sits in the back of his parent's car the way he has done since he was in a car seat. He is eighteen. He will be going off to college next year and is sure this is the last time he will have to make this trip.

Every year he is crammed into the back seat on Christmas day with all the gifts and the family drives to his grandmother's. It is a two-hour drive in which his parents will talk about all the ways this day is going to be horrible. They dread going. They hate buying gifts for people who won't appreciate them. His mother complains that grandma will turn up her nose at the pies she worked hard on. His father dreads sitting with grandpa who just sits and watches TV and says nothing.

Jason knows that the drive home will be filled with complaints about the gifts that they received and "how come she never buys my size" and "didn't I get the same gift last year." Jason makes a vow (again) that he will never do this to his children. He will find a wife and have kids and they will celebrate Christmas the way it's supposed to be celebrated, if he could just figure out what that is.

Right now, he is weighing whether to cancel out on the trip or not.

- Have you ever seen some way in which your parents are just like their parents? In what way(s)?

- How do you want to be most like your parents? Least like your parents? Why?

- Can you relate to Jason's situation? How do we let family problems get in the way of family celebrations? Explain.

- What's the key for keeping sight of the "reason for the season"?

**Romans 8:24
2 Timothy 2:23-26**

- What are Jason's options at this point? What about when he's 18?

RESERVING JUDGMENT

Rene has a friend named Julia. They have been friends for a while and discovered a long time ago that they approached their religious beliefs differently. Rene is Jewish but her parents do not attend a temple. Julia has invited Rene to her church's "Judgment House Experience" this Halloween where ticket holders experience a scene of hell, Satan and demons in horror house fashion.

Julia has been a lot more forceful lately about pushing her beliefs on Rene. Julia calls it witnessing. Rene calls it being pushy.

Julia keeps telling Rene about how many kids are finding Christ because of the Judgment House. "We're scaring the Jesus right into them!" Julia says, laughing at her own joke.

Rene would like to get more serious about her own faith but doesn't want to be a part of Julia's church or be part of anything even close to the "Judgment House Experience." She wishes Julia would just keep her mouth shut about it and they could go back to being friends.

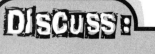

@ What was a scary movie you watched when you were a kid? Recently? Are you scared of them at this moment? Why?

@ What do you think of churches putting on "house of horror" type things like the "Judgment House Experience"? Why? (Ever been to one of these? If so, describe it.)

@ Does it sound like Julia may be going a little overboard in sharing her faith? Why?

@ Do we have a right to judge the way anybody else connects with God? Why?

@ What does it feel like to have someone tell you what to do? Why?

@ Should Julia say nothing about her faith to Rene...just be a good friend to her and "witness" without using words? Why?

Matthew 5:14-16
Ephesians 2:8
Romans 17:15-18

@ Should Rene keep quiet or talk with Julie to let her know her faith-sharing is uncomfortably forceful? How should Julie respond if Rene speaks with her—just keep sharing her faith as she always has, or tone it down a bit? Why?

NO WORD

Kevin wasn't there when his little sister, Caitlin, was kidnapped. It was a crowded playground. His mother took him there when he was little. He had taken his sister himself a few times after he got his driver's license. Every day his mother met her friend Irene at the park and they watched their children play.

Caitlin asked if Irene's daughter, Kimmy, could go to the duck pond. That was the last anybody saw of her. Kimmy came back crying because she couldn't find Caitlin. Every parent in the park began to help look. The police were called. A special team came in and began searching the pond.

It's been six months. No leads. Nothing.

Less than 24 hours later a garbage man from the next town over reported finding a body in a dumpster behind a restaurant. It was Caitlin.

Kevin is devastated. He hopes it will be like it is on television— the pervert will be found and arrested and all loose ends will be tied up quickly.

It's been over two months now. The police still have nothing to go on. No leads. Nothing.

DISCUSS:

@ **What is the worst thing that could happen to you or a loved one right now? What would you do if it happened? Why?**

@ **Job lost his family and wept and the praised God, could you do that? Why?**

@ **Tragedies happen all the time. Is there a reason? Explain.**

@ **Why does God allow bad or tragic things to happen?**

@ **What do you think is going on inside Kevin right now? Why?**

Read: **2 Corinthians 1:3-7
Psalm 22:1-5**

@ **If Kevin asked you why God allowed this to happen, what would you say? Why?**

TAKE UP THE CROSS

It's springtime and nearly Easter. Between school and the fast food place where he works, there are a variety of shops. Kendal enjoys the shops, but none more than the candy shop that sells homemade chocolates. He bought his mother some chocolate-covered strawberries there (her favorite) last Mother's Day.

Kendal has noticed a new display in the window. There, standing in the jelly beans next to the chocolate bunny, is a chocolate Jesus. He's standing there holding a lamb in his arms. At first Kendal had no opinion about it, but the more times he walked by the window the angrier he became.

To Kendal, Jesus should not be used to help commercialize the holiday and he certainly should not be eaten like a chocolate bunny. Kendal started walking on the other side of the street but it still angered him. He wants to go in and buy them all and throw them away. He wants to go in and tell the owner what he thinks about the display, but he hasn't…not yet anyway.

@ Do we go to far with using religion to sell things?

@ Is a chocolate Jesus wrong or a good thing? Wrong to show Santa kneeling at the manger? The Easter Bunny at Jesus' tomb?

@ When someone disrespects Jesus, should we always make an issue of it, or do we sometimes ignore such things? Why?

@ If we never make an issue of disrespect toward Jesus, what could that say about us? Our faith? Why?

@ Should we take any opportunity to show or display our beliefs? Why?

@ Is a cross necklace wrong? Earring? T-Shirt? Tattoo? Where do you draw the line?

**1 Corinthians 15:58
2 Timothy 2:15**

@ What should Kendal do?

ON A MISSION

Angela came back from the youth mission trip on fire. She had a great experience and wanted to get more involved in her church and her community.

The first thing she did was join the mission committee at her church. They approve funds for mission work and schedule volunteers to cook at the homeless shelter once a month. Angela wanted to find a way to increase the amount of money they send to the various organizations they support overseas.

The committee listens to her thoughts and ideas (usually) but then continues to do things the way they've done them for years. She has asked her youth minister for help but he can only sympathize without offering much help.

The church is about to spend seven hundred and fifty thousand dollars on an addition to the sanctuary. Angela has done the math and figured out exactly how many meals that money would by for an orphanage in Haiti and she is appalled. She is planning on going to the next administrative board meeting and asking them to reconsider the spending plan—or at least offer matching funds to the orphanage.

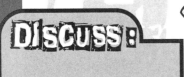

DISCUSS:

@ **Do we have a responsibility to care for "our own" first? Why or why not?**

@ **Is our church more about business or ministry? Why?**

@ **Is it important to be involved in your church? Your community? Why?**

@ **Which should come first, an addition to the sanctuary or money to the orphanage in Haiti? Why?**

@ **Who is *really* in charge at our church?**

Read: Hebrews 10:24-25
Ephesians 4:16
Matthew 28:18-20

@ **How should Angela present this problem to the board?**

SANCTUARY

Two of the guys in Dion's youth group decided to trash the sanctuary. Every kid in the youth group knew about the window in the kitchen that didn't lock. (The youth pointed it out to the new youth minister when she started.)

Evan and Jerry snuck into the church last week and took a baseball bat to the altar. They pulled out the organ pipes, ripped the altar clothes and knocked over the pulpit. They broke several lights and damaged the organ and the sound system.

The worst part is that there seemed to be no reason for the vandalism. Both of the guys had been in a little trouble but never anything serious. Now they had trashed the church.

Both boys were eventually caught and arrested and let go. Rev. Tomlinson decided not to press charges, but the boys have to pay for the vandalism. Everyone seems to want to move on, except Dion. She sees the two sit in church on Sunday and she just wants to scream. She doesn't want them there. She doesn't want them in the youth group. She can't understand why the minister and so many others are willing to just let it go.

DISCUSS:

- Should the minister have pressed charges? Why?

- Should the arrested boys be banned from the church or youth group meetings? Why?

- Within days of a teen shooter gunning down students gathered for a campus Bible study, students stood outside that school holding signs that said "We forgive you _____ (shooter's first name)." What do you think of this? Why?

- How long does it take to forgive someone? How long should it take—should it happen immediately? What's right?

- Whose job is it to forgive in this situation? Is forgetting a part of that? Explain.

- What is "atonement"?

Read:

Ephesians 4:22-24
Proverbs 12:15
Hebrews 7:27

- What should Dion do? What if it happened again?

GREEN

There is a running joke about green M&Ms at Marcie's lunch table. She knows it's always been a "thing" that green M&Ms make you horny. Her mother even mentioned that it was a "thing" when she was a teenager.

But the girls at Marcie's lunch table are taking it to extremes. They've made up poems and songs about green M&Ms. They take little plastic bags of green M&Ms and slip them into the lockers of boys that they think are cute. They wear green clothes every Thursday and chuckle at others who are wearing green but who don't know what it "really means."

Marcie decided to do them all one better. She likes to make her own t-shirts from iron-on's and images that she downloads from the Internet. She made a t-shirt that had two large green M&Ms strategically placed on the front of the shirt. Her friends thought the shirt was very funny. Her homeroom teacher did not. Marcie was sent to the office to call her mother to bring in a different shirt for her to wear.

@ Is Marcie's shirt funny or indecent? Both? Why?

@ What would you do if you were Marcie's mother? Why?

@ Could the shirt be taken as offensive? Explain. Would you think it was funny or offensive?

@ What harm could there be in wearing a silly shirt? Explain.

@ Did the homeroom teacher overreact? Explain.

@ If you were the principal what would your "guideline" be for offensive shirts or material?

 **Philippians 4:8
Matthew 6:25
Isaiah 23:16-23**

@ If Marcie is a Christian, how should she respond to calls for her to change her shirt? (Does it matter whether or not she's a Christian?) Why?

STANDING UP

Mr. Furges has been a teacher for nearly 40 years. He has unusual methods of teaching but most of the student trust and respect him. He is tough, but fair—no student could ever say they didn't get the grade they deserved.

Mr. Furges has a method of dealing with careless mistakes that many teachers and parents find unacceptable. Mr. Furges went to school when the dunce cap was still allowed. If a student makes a careless mistake on a test one time, Mr. Furges will circle it in red. If the student makes a stupid mistake a second time, Mr. Furges will make the student stand on his or her chair and announce to the class "I am an idiot."

Chris made a big mistake on the latest test. Mr. Furges always throws in an easy question "Just so no one can get a zero." This week's question was "What are the colors of the American flag?" Chris wrote "red, blue and yellow." She doesn't remember why.

Mr. Furges has deemed this worthy of an "I am an idiot" punishment and tells Chris to stand and make the announcement. Chris politely refuses. Mr. Furges tells her that she will or she will fail the test. Chris again politely refuses. Mr. Furges fails her.

○ **What do you think of Mr. Furges' "I am an idiot" punishment? Why?**

○ **Is a student entitled to some dignity even if they make a dumb mistake? Why?**

○ **Do teachers have a right to use whatever methods they find most useful to get results? Why? Is Mr. Furges going overboard? Explain.**

○ **Who stands to lose the most here, Mr. Furges or Chris? Why?**

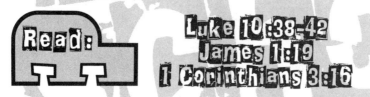

Read:

**Luke 10:38-42
James 1:19
1 Corinthians 3:16**

○ **If you were Chris, what would you do? Why?**

RESULTS

As a homework assignment, Kathy was asked to write an essay about the person who most influenced her life. Her friends at the lunch table all talked about role models and people they look up to, but Kathy can only keep coming back to one thought. Her mother is the biggest influence in her life, but not for positive reasons.

Kathy's mother is very critical of everything she does ("good is not good enough"), kept close track of her every move, volunteered in every group that Kathy becomes a part of, and used to sit directly behind her during piano lessons until the teacher said she had to leave. (Kathy's mom got a new piano teacher.) Kathy tells her friends "Everything that I am is a result of my mother and it's not good."

Her friends tell her to make something up and turn in the assignment. Kathy agrees that this is probably the best move but she can't get over the idea that the person she is becoming is due mostly to negative influences.

DISCUSS:

@ Who is your biggest influence...positive or negative?

@ Who decides whom you will turn out to be—you and your choices or the influence of others on your life? Why?

@ What has been the biggest hurdle in your life so far? How have you dealt with it? Why?

@ How is Kathy's mom's brand of parenting affecting her?

Read: Proverbs 27:17
Proverbs 3:5-6
Jeremiah 1:6-8

@ If you were Kathy, what sort of essay would you write—truth or fiction? Why?

CONFLICT

Lyle is the only one in his school who won't wear the flag pin that was passed out in homeroom. It was supposed to be an effort to show support for the troops overseas. Lyle is not unpatriotic, but he doesn't understand why the troops are fighting in the first place. He knows half the kids in the school couldn't point out the country where the troops are on a map. They're wearing the flag because it's cool to be wearing a flag right now.

Lyle believes that fighting is wrong, but understand the idea of a "just war." He just doesn't see the point of sending American's over to foreign lands so that the average American can spend a little less at the gas pump.

He has refused to wear the pin. Now everyone in school is staring at him. He has been threatened by several guys who tell him he is communist. Lyle wonders if any of them can spell "communist" let alone know what it means.

The school is not that big and soon everyone is talking about it. Lyle's teacher has taken him aside and said that there are times and places to rock the boat—but this probably isn't one of them.

@ Is Lyle simply rocking the boat or standing up for his views on the flag pin issue? Explain.

@ It's just a pin. Should Lyle simply put it on and shut up?

@ Talk about a time in your life where following the crowd was the best course of action at the time. (Fire drills don't count!)

@ What lessons is Lyle learning about patriotism and freedom of expression? What's the bigger lesson? Explain.

@ When is war justified? Explain.

@ The prime minister of France once said, "War is the acceptance of failure." What did he mean?

Proverbs 2:1-9
Romans 12:18
Ecclesiastes 3:1-8

@ Should Lyle put the pin on or leave it off? Would you? Why?

MOST LIKELY

Geoff graduated last week and was voted "Most Likely to Succeed" by his peers and teachers. He has a college lined up for the fall and a summer job that keeps him indoors and well paid.

For right now he has a week in which to do nothing. His father seems to think this is a week to get some work done on the house. The day after graduation Geoff's dad told him he would be taking out some old shrubs and putting in some new flowers for his mother. Then the back fence would need to be painted. Then the garage must become less an illustration of the chaos theory.

Geoff doesn't understand why he can't take this last opportunity to simply do nothing. His teachers and friends seem him as the "most likely" but his father seems to think this is one last chance to use him as a slave.

@ Is Geoff entitled to some time off? Explain.

@ What is Geoff's responsibility to his family and their home? Why?

@ Is this a "Geoff" thing or a "Dad" thing? Explain.

@ Do you parents see you differently than everyone else? Why?

Genesis 2:2
Romans 12:3-5
Ecclesiastes 2:17-24

@ How would you talk about this to your dad if you were Geoff?

TAKE NOTES/MAKE NOTES

OPENING UP

Nick remembers when his grandma was one of those grandmas who bakes cookies and always had candy in her purse. She was there with a hug and a kiss and would be the first one to tell her grandchildren how perfect they were.

Nick's grandfather passed away six years ago and since then Nick's grandmother has become angry and bitter. Despite efforts of her family and friends to turn her personality around she finds no joy in anyone or anything anymore. The family has now come to dread holidays and family visits because grandma will do nothing but complain.

Grandma has decided she needs to clean out her garage and asked if Nick would take a Saturday and drive up for a day of cleaning. Nick told his mother he didn't want to go, but his mother talked him into it. Now Nick has spent the last six hours sweating and huffing boxes around while his grandmother sits in a lawn chair and offers "instruction" on where and how things are to be moved.

While moving one box, the bottom broke out and years worth of cheap plastic knick-knacks spilled on the floor. "Well that was just brilliant!" his grandmother shouted. Nick turned to her and in a rage he had never used on anyone said, "Will you get off my back you bitter old (*)&%^#!" Grandma's jaw dropped and she started to cry.

@ **Why the drastic change in Nick's grandma?**

@ **What are some tips for Nick on controlling his anger? Explain.**

@ **What would you do if you were grandma? Why?**

@ **Do you know someone who desperately needs to hear some "truth," but no one will give it, because they're afraid to hurt their feelings?**

@ **Who was the last person to give you a dope slap? (Physical or verbal)**

@ **How can you "take it back," when you say the wrong thing?**

Read:

Ephesians 4:29-32
Psalm 139:23-24
Hebrews 12:15

@ **What should the next thing out of Nick's mouth be? How can you "take it back" when you say the wrong thing? Why?**

NO GIFTS

Yolanda has been in the youth group now for two years. She started attending when a friend invited her and now shows up to all events. She loves the youth director and enjoys her talks and lessons. This week, her youth director challenged the youth to use their spiritual gifts for the church. Artists are asked to design bulletin covers. Athletes are asked to lead games for the church picnic. Writers are asked to create liturgy.

Yolanda believes that every person has gifts from God but she has no idea what hers are. She really wants to take this assignment seriously and not just sign on somewhere to put in her time, but she doesn't know what to do. She likes all music, and arts, and is good with numbers, but doesn't feel that any of these are truly spiritual gifts.

◎ **Do you think Michael Jordan, the first time he got his hands on a basketball, ran down the court and slam-dunked it? What did it take for him to learn to dunk? How might this apply to you finding or growing in your spiritual gifts?**

◎ **What do you think makes a gift "spiritual"?**

◎ **What might be Yolanda's spiritual gift? Why?**

**I Corinthians 12:4-13
Matthew 25:15-40**

◎ **What can Yolanda do to discover her spiritual gift(s)?**

TAKE NOTES/MAKE NOTES

SPIRITUAL GIFTS, SERVING THE CHURCH, FAITHFULNESS

THREATS OF VIOLENCE, BULLYING, DISCIPLINE

TURNING PAGES

Marion's favorite movie is *Carrie*. She says the book is better than the movie and is constantly seen with a beaten, dog-eared copy of the book in her backpack. She's told several people that she especially likes the scene where all the "perfect" kids in the school die in a fire. Marion is unattractive, keeps very much to herself and has only a few friends.

One girl in the school named Michelle has been riding Marion's back since junior high. Michelle constantly makes fun of Marion, laughing at her and baiting her. Anyone who pays attention could see the similarities between Marion and the girl in the novel) Michelle spent a recent lunch period calling out, "Suuuuuueeee," and making pig noises in Marion's direction.

Marion responded by ripping the cover off the book and writing a vulgar death threat (heavier on vulgar than threat) 50 times on the backside. She slides this into Michelle's locker. Michelle promptly takes it to the principal, who expels Marion for threatening violence.

@ Are we, as a culture, too sensitive since the Columbine High School tragedy? Explain.

@ Have you ever been bullied? How did you respond?

@ Why do you think Michelle is so relentless in her bullying? How long should a person have to put up with taunting, verbal abuse, and bullying? Why?

@ What would you do if you were Marion's parents?

Proverbs 18:21
1 Thessalonians 5:15

@ If you were Marion and were called to the principal's office, what would you say or do? Why?

WAITRESS WANTED

Anna took a job as a waitress at a small diner in town. She works mostly weekends and is occasionally called to fill in on the dinner rush if someone calls in sick. Her feet hurt and she is tired, but the money is good and she finds that she actually feels pretty good about herself after putting in a hard days work.

On Saturday mornings, Mr. James comes in. He is in his seventies and constantly gives waitresses a hard time. Mostly, he makes sexual comments and invites waitresses to come to his house. A few of the waitresses complained to the manager, who told Mr. James to knock it off, but it wasn't very effective.

Anna is the newest waitress and has been assigned to Mr. James as a sort of initiation. Anna ignores his comments about her breasts and butt. She attempts to laugh it off when he invites her to his home. After several weeks at Anna's station Mr. James leaves Anna a hundred dollar tip. No one is more shocked than she is.

Immediately, the waitresses start asking her what she did to get such a generous tip. One waitress even said she has an obligation to share the tip with the rest of them since they had to deal with Mr. James long before she even got hired.

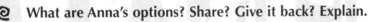

⚛ **What are Anna's options? Share? Give it back? Explain.**

⚛ **Instead of being happy for her getting the huge tip, the other waitresses seem to be jealous or angry with Anna. Why is this?**

⚛ **Did Anna do anything wrong? Explain.**

⚛ **Have you ever been falsely accused?**

⚛ **Why do some people not want others to have something they can't have?**

Read: **Proverbs 20:11**
Romans 5:1-4

⚛ **What should Anna do with the tip? Why?**

DRUGS, DEATH, HONESTY

LEFT UNSAID

Gwen has been good friends with Shauna since the second grade. They've hung out together, studied together and "scoped" boys at the mall every Saturday for the last six months.

Recently, a guy named Brad has been coming to their table at lunch and inviting them to his house on Saturdays where he and some friends get high. Gwen and Shauna refuse and Gwen doesn't think about it again.

On Monday morning, the police are at school. On Saturday night, Brad was found dead in his room. The principal asked that anyone with any information to come forward. Gwen knows that Shauna was not with her at the mall on Saturday.

When she told Shauna she was going to go the principal and tell them about Brad's invitations, Shauna said it would be better if they just left it all alone.

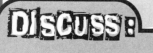

@ What's the worst thing you ever had to do in order to make something "right"? Explain.

@ How strong is the "code of silence" of your friends—what kinds of concerns and crises do you not share with adults? What concerns and crises would you share with adults? Explain.

@ How would Gwen's going forward help? Is she jeopardizing a friendship by going forward? Explain.

@ Should Shauna be the one to say something if she knows something? Why?

Isaiah 3:10-11

@ What would you do in Gwen's situation?

WOMEN'S RIGHTS

Debbie and Pat have been active in "women's activities" at the school since the school year began. Debbie formed a feminist campus club and has begun writing a feminist column for the school newspaper. She spends a lot of free time working to advance feminist causes. She has a pretty intense feminist agenda.

When the class election came up and ballots were passed out in class, Pat watched as Debbie went down the column and marked a vote for every girl who was running for everything—with no apparent thought.

Pat looked at the list and saw at least two girls who she felt weren't even close to being qualified to hold the position they were running for. She mentioned this to Debbie, who simply said, "Better a stupid girl in the job than any guy at all."

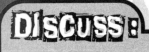

*   What are your thoughts on Debbie's perspective? Why?

    *   Are Debbie's views a problem? What if she feels that she is simply doing what guys have done to girls for years? Explain.

*   How might Debbie become what she was fighting against? Explain.

    *   In what ways do you identify with Debbie? Pat? Why?

Romans 12:3
1 John 4:20

*   If you were Pat what would you do? Would you say something to Debbie? What? Why?

TAKE NOTES/MAKE NOTES

JUST WORDS?

Doreen's homeroom class has a new teacher. Mrs. Davenport has taken maternity leave, so they will have Mr. Kratowski for the rest of the year.

On his first day, Mr. Kratowski took attendance, calling out names and looking at each student to put each face with a name. He called Doreen's name, looked up and said, "Wow, that is a really bad dye job!"

The other students laughed and Mr. Kratowski continued taking attendance. He didn't say anything negative about any other students. For some reason, Doreen hasn't been able to get his comment out of her head all day.

She thought maybe she should go and ask for an apology or say something to Mr. Kratowksi, but her friend Meg says she should just let it go.

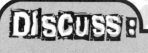

© Has anything like this ever happened to you? Tell us about it.

© Why do you think Mr. Kratowski made this rude comment? Explain.

© Can a tongue be "tamed"? How could Mr. Kratowski have avoided saying what he said? Explain.

© What are Doreen's options? Explain.

1 Peter 3:9

© If you were Doreen, what would you do?

TAKE NOTES/MAKE NOTES

UN-STEADY

Neville wants to break up with his girlfriend, Rona. They've been dating for six months and he doesn't feel they're having fun anymore. His sisters both told him that if he broke up with her on the phone or by email he would be the biggest jerk in the world. So he invited Rona to lunch.

They went to a little burger place they had gone to before. He told her quietly that he didn't think they needed to see each other anymore.

Rona began to sob. She told him that she thought he was taking her out to their "special place" so he would ask her to go steady.

She suddenly began shouting and cursing at him in the restaurant. Finally she threw a large drink in his face and stormed out of the restaurant.

The next day in school all the girls in his class glared at him. He found horrible things written on his locker and a girl tried to trip him when he was carrying his lunch tray.

© **Did Neville do anything wrong? Did Rona? Explain.**

© **Neville is now between a rock and a hard place. What advice would you give him? Why?**

© **What advice would you give Rona?**

© **Reverse the roles...what if Rona had broken up with Neville this way...would it have gone any better?**

Psalm 37:5-8

© **What could Neville have done differently? Explain.**

© **What should he do now? Why?**

TAKE NOTES/MAKE NOTES

OUT OF THE DARK

Randy thought he was mostly rid of his brother, Jack. They had fought a lot like brothers do and gotten along just like brothers do. But ultimately, Randy always felt like he was somehow lost in his big brother's shadow.

Jack went to college last year and Randy suddenly felt he had come into his own. His grades went up. His attitude improved. He started making extra money babysitting for a neighbor with three sons who couldn't keep a sitter. Even his parents commented on how much he had grown. Randy believed that it was due, at least in part, to finally being able to be seen as his own person rather than as Jack's little brother.

Jack showed up at the door for Thanksgiving break with all his belongings. He announced that he had flunked out and that college wasn't for him. Randy suddenly felt that he was in a time warp. In no time, his brother was once again bossing him around and getting all of the attention.

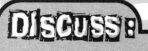

DISCUSS:

@ Have you ever been in someone else's shadow? Are you still there, or did you get out? Explain.

@ What is Randy going through right now? Explain.

@ Who's got the bigger problem, Randy, his brother, or his parents? Why?

@ How might Randy bring this up to his brother? Explain.

@ Should Randy bring the subject up to his parents? How?

Read:

Galatians 5:22-23

@ What are some other options that are open to Randy?

TAKE NOTES/MAKE NOTES

154

HOME COOKING?

Amanda's mother can't cook. She reads the recipes, but nothing ever seems to come out right. Ever since she was small, Amanda remembers nothing but easy, instant, "no-time-in-the-kitchen" meals.

About six months ago, Amanda's mother asked her if she would be willing to make something for the monthly church potluck lunch. (Her mother usually stopped at a bakery on the way to church, bought cookies, removed them from the box and wrapped them on a plate.) Amanda dug through the cookbooks, found a recipe and made a delicious green bean casserole.

A month later, her mother asked her again and again the month after that. Last month, Amanda was sitting with her family, when someone came over and complimented her mother on the wonderful Chinese chicken dish she brought to the dinner. Amanda was about to say "thank you," when her mother said, "Thank you. It's a favorite at our house." The woman walked away and Amanda stared at her mother. Her mother simply said "What?"

DISCUSS:

@ **Have you ever had someone take credit for something you did? (Good or Bad) Explain.**

@ **Technically, did Amanda's mother lie? Did she do anything else wrong? Explain.**

@ **How far does a "little white lie" have to go before it becomes a "big honkin' whopper"?**

@ **If you were Amanda, would you cook again? Why?**

@ **Do you do something you love because you want to be praised or because you love to do it?**

Read:

Leviticus 19:11-13

@ **How should Amanda address this with her mother? Explain.**

WELCOME?

David has just moved to town and his family has been "church shopping." They've finally found a church they like.

It's not too big and not too small. The service seems to be a nice balance of traditional and contemporary. The minister seems nice and the sermons are short, to the point and relevant to life. David decided to check out the youth group.

As he approached the door, three students from the youth group met him, said "hi," then immediately asked David if he was saved. David wasn't sure how to respond. When the youth leader started the meeting, he asked if there were any visitors. One of the girls mentioned that David was visiting and that he was unsaved and needed Jesus. The youth minister immediately led a prayer that David would find Jesus and that his soul would be saved from hell.

As the meeting continued, David began to feel shunned and out of place. No one really talked to him. He didn't know their songs, prayers or creeds, nor did he know how to find verses in the Bible.

By the time the meeting was over, David was pretty sure this would be his last visit.

DISCUSS:

- ✪ How typical do you think this story is?

- ✪ When have you felt out of place or unwelcome, like David? Tell about it.

- ✪ Why do some people use the faith as a sort of license to straighten others out or to get others to be like them? Explain.

- ✪ Why do you think the youth group members acted as they did? Explain.

- ✪ Who were the Pharisees? How did they stay in power?

- ✪ Who gets to say who is saved and who isn't?

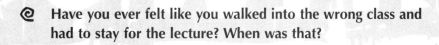
e Have you ever felt like you walked into the wrong class and had to stay for the lecture? When was that?

e What could the youth group members have done differently to actually draw David into their group

e How did Jesus tell us to bring others into the kingdom?

Ephesians 5:1-2

e Talk about what you would do if you were David.

TAKE NOTES/MAKE NOTES

A TEAM OF ONE

Mark is an incredible baseball pitcher. The problem is that Mark is starting to feel like he's too good. He's thrown several no-hitter games and it's gone to his head. His teammates are accusing Mark of having an ego problem.

Rather than being happy for him, his fellow pitchers are starting to get mad because they don't get the opportunities to "show their stuff." Mark's coach has his eyes on the state championship and won't put anyone else in to pitch until the team is clearly ahead.

Mark is tempted to fake an injury just so he can give himself some bench time and see how the team flounders without him.

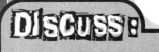

@ What about the body of Christ, is it all about the body or the individual? Why?

@ What would happen if you little finger didn't want to be part of the hand anymore because it wasn't a thumb? How is Mark's situation similar?

@ What do you think of Mark's plan to fake an injury to watch his teammates struggle without him? What good would this accomplish? What bad? Explain.

@ If the team wins...isn't that what's important? Is that being a "team"?

@ Explain the phrase "a love of the game?"

@ What would happen if you little finger didn't want to be part of the hand anymore because it wasn't a thumb?

@ Doesn't Mark have an obligation to get into a college and make his (and his father's) dreams come true? Is there anything wrong with that? Talk about that.

Romans 12:4-10

@ What should Mark do? The coach? The other players?

PLAN "B"

Anthony is a star football player. Though he excels on the football field, he has always struggled academically. His philosophy is "I'm going to be a professional football player, I'll do just what I have to do to get by in school." Sometimes he doesn't do enough to get by.

He is barely eligible to play sports in school and he doesn't care. Anthony's mother worries because he lacks self-motivation to study and because, as to his future, he is putting all his "eggs" in one "basket"—football.

She can see her son has a gift, but what if something happens? What if he suffers an injury? What if scouts decide not to take him? She loves her son and supports his dream, but she's worried that he has no "plan B" if his football plan falls through.

@ Considering how few professional football players there are and how many people there are competing for those positions, should Anthony have a plan "B"? Explain.

@ Does God answer all prayers? If you say "God, I want to be a pro football player," will God make me one?

@ Should we follow our dream at all costs, or should we have a plan "B" in life? Will a plan "B" keep us from following our dream 100 percent? Why?

@ Should Anthony's mom be more supportive of him in his dream? Why?

@ If the Bible says, "Don't worry about tomorrow," does that mean we just put it all in Jesus' hands and forget about it? Explain.

@ If you could do anything you wanted for a career what would it be? What is plan "B"?

Jeremiah 29:11
Colossians 3:23

@ What would you do if you were Anthony?

THE FACE OF JESUS

Brenda loves her church. She has grown up there and has participated in all activities since she was a child. She attended vacation Bible school until she was old enough to help teach and now she teaches a class every summer.

The church recently commissioned an artist to paint on the wall of the sanctuary, the ascension of Christ to heaven. As the portrait begins to take shape, people are amazed at the beauty of it. The pastor even plans his sermons around the progress of the painting.

Brenda sees something in the face of Jesus that no one else has seen. Recognition. She knows the face from somewhere.

She checks the artist's website and finds several sketches and paintings of the same model. One of the notes beneath the picture identifies the model.

Brenda recognizes the model's face because he is a model for an "adult website" that Brenda has visited on more than a few occasions.

@ Consider the classic painting, "The Last Supper," by da Vinci. If someone told you that the model for Jesus in that work had a shameful lifestyle, should the painting still be considered a classic? Should the painting be destroyed?

@ Jesus was all about forgiveness. In that spirit, should forgiveness be extended to the model and the matter of the use of his image be overlooked? Why?

@ What's the upside for Brenda letting someone know about the issue? The downside?

@ If you were in Brenda's place, and said nothing, could you worship there without feeling guilty? Explain.

@ How might God be testing Brenda?

Hebrews 4:16
1 Corinthians 12:27
Acts 17:24-29

@ If you were Brenda, should you let someone know about the issue? How? Why?

WHAT HAPPENS

Shawn is in the 7th grade and old enough, at last, to join the church youth group. Shawn envied his older brother when he was in youth group because of all the fun stuff they did. Now he is in the church on the first night of the new school year.

There are more than fifty junior-higher's running around in the parking lot. Some are tossing a Frisbee. Others are playing kickball with an adult leader. A lot of kids are just standing around talking.

Shawn walks up to a couple guys he knows. They are arguing about what happens when you put a can of soda in a microwave. Shawn walks on when they don't seem to notice he is there.

About an hour later a smoke alarm goes off in the church. Someone has put a metal can in the microwave in the kitchen. Evidently the microwave (older than most of the students) sparks wildly before setting a stack of nearby dishtowels on fire.

An adult leader uses a fire extinguisher and put out the fire. The leaders are wondering which youth group members to "talk to" about the can in the microwave.

@ Why do we do things we know are stupid at the time we are doing them? Tell about the most stupid thing you've done.

@ Are certain kinds of behavior excusable because you are a "teenager"? Should they be?

@ If Shawn tells a leader who put the can in the microwave, what might happen? If he doesn't tell, what might happen? Why?

@ If the church had caught fire and suffered serious damage would that would that be more of a reason for Shawn to tell a leader or more of a reason to stay quiet? Why?

Ephesians 5:8-11

@ What should Shawn do?

PART OF THE GAME

Stephan has baseball in his blood. His father and all his uncles played, as did his grandfather, great-grandfather and even his brothers. He started in little league and now he plays for the high school team. All the relatives agree that as good at baseball as they all are, Stephan has a gift for baseball and an unbelievable pitching arm. Stephan's father dreams of sitting behind home plate during a World Series as his son pitched a no-hitter.

Stephan's coach told his parents that Stephan's ability could get him into any college in the country. Even over the last year, he has improved dramatically, gaining both power and control. Stephan's team is in first place and college scouts are taking notice.

A month ago, Stan noticed soreness in his throwing arm. After several games, the pain only got worse, so Stephan went to the family doctor. The doctor recommended some tests. Stephan was diagnosed with cancer. His throwing arm would have to be amputated.

Stephan's family has always been religious and this has caused a crisis of faith. Stephan can't believe that a God of love would take back such a wonderful gift just has he was beginning to get the full use of it.

@ **When this kind of tragedy happens, what do people typically say about why it has happened? Explain.**

@ **What is Stephan going through right now? His family? Why?**

@ **If you were Stephan's friend, how would you react to all this? Why?**

@ **If Stephan asked you why this happened or what good could possibly come out of this, what would you say? Why?**

@ **What is Stephan's gift?**

@ **Where is Stephan's gift?**

@ **Why do you think God doesn't show us the plan?**

@ **Is there a way to know for sure if you are using God's gifts?**

@ **Would God ever take a gift back? Explain your theory.**

Romans 5:1-4 and 8:28

@ **What would you do if you were Stephan?**

RED AND BLUE

Rose has a best friend named Nancy. They are in the ninth grade and have been best friends since the sixth grade, when they shared a locker.

Nancy had a boyfriend for over a year. Three months ago, at the beginning of the school year, her boyfriend dumped her for someone else. Nancy has been heartbroken ever since. Every time she and Rose are together, Nancy winds up talking about him. She show's Rose new poems she's written about him and her heartache.

Rose is just about fed up with hearing about Tom. She's ready to tell Nancy to "get over it already." Last night, Nancy called Rose to sing her the latest song she wrote about her break up with Tom. When Nancy put the phone down to play her guitar Rose hung her line up. Now they are sitting together outside school waiting for the morning bell.

@ **Ever had a friend this heartbroken? What does a heartbroken friend need most? Explain.**

@ **If it's your best friend, aren't you obligated to listen even when you don't feel like listening? Why?**

@ **What's the upside if Nancy tells Rose to "get over it"? The downside? As a friend, is there ever a time to say "get over it"? Explain.**

@ How do guys and girls handle break-ups differently? Explain.

@ **Is there one person you are destined to be with? How likely is it that you will meet that person in ninth grade? What does this tell you?**

Proverbs 12:18; 27:6

@ **If you were Rose, how would you finally address this problem with Nancy?**

NEW CREATION

Walter will be the first one to tell you that last year he was a screw-up. He didn't turn in homework. He spent a great deal of time in detention. He fought with his parents constantly.

This year things have never been better for him. He finally feels like he has his act together. Everything seems to be going well except his relationship with his dad. His dad still remembers the arguments, the grades, and the attitude.

Walter really feels like his whole life has turned around, but nothing he does seems to convince his dad. Good grades mean he's cheating. A good mood means he's on something. A bad mood means he's on something.

Walter has found himself giving the attitude back to his dad, at which point his dad just turns to his mother and says, "See, I told you."

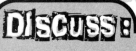

Discuss:

@ **Why is Walter's dad having such a hard time believing he has really changed? Will time help? Explain.**

@ **Is it possible to change someone's perception of you? Should you even try? Explain.**

@ **If someone repeatedly lies to you or is mean to you, how hard is it to believe they've changed? To forgive them? Why?**

Read:

Philippians 2:12-15

@ **Is it possible for Walter to win over his dad? How? Explain.**

TAKE NOTES/MAKE NOTES

DEVELOPMENTS

Oliver is graduating in six months and already has a scholarship to a state college about two hours from home. Oliver wants to major in art, but his parents are insistent that he take something he can "actually use" and take art as a minor.

Oliver is attending a photographic exhibit at a museum and winds up talking to the photographer for over two hours. By the end of the conversation the photographer has offered him a job as an assistant on a photographic shoot in Africa. They won't leave until Oliver is out of school and they will be back in six months.

Oliver is thinking it's a dream come true. He's already made a list of all his parents' objections and another list of answers to those objections. Oliver has invited the photographer over to his house tonight, but has not yet mentioned anything about the offer to his parents.

DISCUSS:

@ How far would you go to make your parents happy? Would you give up on a dream? Explain.

@ If you were a parent, how far would you go to make your kid's dreams come true? Why?

@ How important is it for Oliver to pray about his decision that concerns six months of his life? Why?

@ How has Oliver shown his maturity? His immaturity? Explain.

@ If you were Oliver's parents, would you let him go on the trip? With or without conditions? Why?

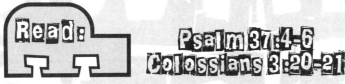

Read: Psalm 37:4-6
Colossians 3:20-21

@ If you were Oliver, what would you do?

DREAMS, FUTURE, HEARING GOD

NO STOPPING

Betsy firmly believes in a "balanced life." By this she means equal amounts of work and play, nutritional and junk foods, laughter and sorrow. There's a time to move fast and a time to stand still. A time to work and a time to "smell the roses."

Betsy's mother, on the other hand, is a workaholic. She leaves for work most days before Betsy goes to school. She gets home, cooks dinner, cleans the house and then goes out to attend one of several different community activities where she is a member of a board or committee. Even at church Betsy's mother is known as "the woman who never sits."

The problem is that since Betsy's mother has so much going on that she cannot stand to see Betsy sitting. She doesn't even like Betsy to stretch out on the couch and read a book when it's a perfectly nice day. If it's raining Betsy's mother thinks Betsy should be cleaning the house.

Betsy understands her mother grew up this way but she also knows her mother is going to exhaust herself (plus her mom can get pretty grouchy when she's tired). When Betsy expresses concern her mom simply says that if Betsy would do more, she could rest. One day her mom's grouchiness and demands for Betsy to do more boil over. Her mother and she threatens to throw out the TV, burn the video games, and to force Betsy to get a part-time job.

DISCUSS:

@ **Workaholics can tend to have little patience for those who are not similarly wired. Have you ever known anyone who "can't sit down"? What's it like to spend time with them? Explain.**

@ **Is there a danger in "stopping to smell the roses?" In being a workaholic? Explain.**

@ **For a workaholic and a "stop and smell the roses" type to get along, what must they both do? Why?**

@ **Are you more like Betsy or her mom? Is either one of these the best way to be? Why?**

Read:

Proverbs 6:6-11; 13:4

@ **How can Betsy and her mom work this out? What can Betsy do to live with her mother's workaholic expectations?**

SAME OLD, SAME OLD

Sam wants things to quit changing on him or at least to slow down a little. In the past three years, Sam has moved two times. He has been at three different schools. His parents divorced. His youth pastor with whom he had become close was fired. The school switched his homeroom twice since school started. His voice is changing. His older sister went to college. His mother is already dating some guy from work. It seems like nothing has stayed the same in his life for more than a month. Everything changes.

Sam is already planning an adulthood that will include one house, one job, and one wife. Nothing will change. Ever.

Meanwhile, Sam finds that he is reluctant to make friends, because he remembers the pain of leaving friends behind. He has made no effort to get to know his neighbors. Nor does he attend youth group regularly (again, doesn't want to get too close). He doesn't want to know his mom's new boyfriend, because what if it doesn't work out? He misses his older sister. He has never felt more lonelier.

@ Which do you long for the most: same old, same old dependable routine, or; change and new experiences? Why?

@ Sam is planning an adulthood without change. Is this possible? Why?

@ As people get older, they like things to stay the same. Why?

@ What is the purpose of change? Explain.

@ Do you understand Sam's loneliness and his reluctance to develop close friendships? Explain.

@ Is there anything wrong with the life Sam is thinking of? Explain.

@ Is it a "legitimate" idea?

@ Would you rather have a life that is full of extreme highs and extreme lows or a life that pretty much flows along on an even keel.?

@ Do you think certain people do better with change? Why?

@ Who handles change better, men or women?

@ Why does it seem like older people want things to stay the same?

@ Have you ever heard the phrase "the devil you know is better than the devil you don't know"? What does it mean? Is it true?

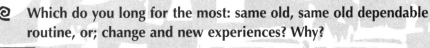

Read: **Romans 5:1-5**
Philippians 4:12-13

@ How will Sam overcome his feelings of loneliness and gain contentment even in his "ever-changing" circumstances?

DISTANCE

Shannon and his family moved to Arizona two years ago. Shannon missed a lot of things about his home, but mostly he missed his grandfather. He had grown up next door to his grandfather and considered him to be his best friend. Yesterday the call came that Shannon's grandfather had died.

Shannon wants to attend the funeral to have one last chance to say goodbye to his best friend. But Shannon's dad is starting up a new business and money is very tight. Shannon's mom spent the day on the Internet trying to track down cheap flights and finally came up with the solution that Shannon's dad alone will fly home for the funeral. She and Shannon will stay behind.

Shannon is devastated that he will not make the trip.

@ **What is the purpose of a funeral? Are they necessary? Explain.**

@ **How would you want to say goodbye to dying loved ones? Why?**

@ **How would you want to say goodbye if you were the one dying? Why?**

@ **Would you rather that your last "visual" of your best friend be through the window of a car driving away, or of them in a coffin?**

@ **Should Shannon's parents do whatever it takes to get him to his grandfather's funeral? Why?**

@ **Is it important for Shannon to have closure on his relationship with his grandfather? Why?**

 **Jeremiah 31:13
Revelation 21:4
John 14:1-4
Isaiah 40:29-31
Job 2:13**

@ **What would you do if you were Shannon?**

SCORE

Doreen is the highest scoring player on her school's volleyball team. Though the volleyball thing is important to Doreen, she is most excited about going into the Peace Corps after graduation.

Doreen's youth group is going to Haiti on a mission trip this year to help build a church. The youth minister has called a mandatory meeting for everyone planning to go on the trip. The meeting is scheduled for the same day as a volleyball game. Every player is allowed to miss only one game per season. Doreen must choose between the church meeting or the volleyball game.

Doreen chooses to attend the meeting. After the meeting, Doreen returns home and plays the messages on her machine. An angry friend is calling to let her know their team lost the game—in fact, it was a shut-out. Her friend closes the message with, "I hope you're happy."

@ **What is loyalty?**

@ **Who are you most loyal to? Why?**

@ **Is church more important than school? Why?**

@ **Rank these in order of importance in your life:**
___ School
___ Church
___ God
___ Friends
___ Family
Explain.

@ **Would you have gone to the meeting or the game? Why?**

@ **How would you react if you were on Doreen's team?**

Proverbs 17:17
Matthew 6:33
1 Timothy 4:14

@ **What should Doreen do now?**

STAYING PUT

Gary was traveling with his church youth group to Haiti. While there, they helped build a church. The trip went great—a real spiritual mountaintop experience for all. Their flight from Haiti to Miami went fine but then they got stranded when their flight from Miami was canceled.

Dave, the youth leader, said it would probably be a few hours, but they were to stay put while he found the customer service counter and made other arrangements. Everybody was wiped out and some were grouchy. Dave knew he had to do what he could to get everyone flying, fast.

Gary felt like he was being treated like a child and had an hour to kill. He didn't stay put, but decided to go for a walk instead. All during the trip he had questioned the rules and second-guessed guessed leaders' decisions. He had been spoken to a number of times by leaders to just do what was asked—he was wearing leaders out.

He explored gift shops and found the observation deck. About 30 minutes later he bought himself a coffee and sat down. Several minutes later, Dave sat down next to him and sighed heavily. His voice was calm, but Gary knew he was angry. "I told you to stay put."

Gary said, "I just wanted a coffee."

"I had us set up on another flight," Dave said. "But we missed it. I couldn't find my whole group because you were missing. I booked us on the next flight, but that doesn't leave for another six hours. You'll want to come with me now. The rest of the group would like to speak with you."

DISCUSS:

- Was what happened with Gary an accident? Why?

- How would you describe Gary's actions and attitude during the trip? Why does he feel like having rules to follow is being treated "like a child"?

- Should Dave, the youth leader, be angry? Should the group be angry? Would you be? Why?

- Was what happened with Gary just an accident that should just be quickly forgiven? Why?

@ **What is the responsibility of the individual as part of the group?**

@ **What is the difference between forgiving and forgetting?**

 **Read:**

Hebrews 13:17
1 Corinthians 12:25-26
Psalm 51
1 Peter 4:8

@ **What would you do if you were Dave? If you were Gary? Why?**

TAKE NOTES/MAKE NOTES

IN THE CARDS

Dontay and his youth group were on a mission trip to Nashville, Tennessee. They spent most of the week working in a homeless shelter. Dontay and six others planted a garden and painted a room that would be a playroom for little kids.

At the end of their trip, they were given a few hours to explore downtown Nashville as long as they stayed in groups of five.

Dontay loved watching the street performers who played music and sang as tourists tossed coins and bills into their instrument cases. Dontay spotted a woman sitting at a card table. A cardboard sign read "Madame Lesosa. Tarot readings $10. Know your future."

In Dontay's church, crystal balls, tarot cards and even a magic eight ball were considered to be tools of the devil. As everyone else watched, Dontay paid his money and sat down at the table. Madame Lesosa had him cut the cards, then she laid them out on the table to begin to read.

Some group members were visibly upset and went quickly to tell the youth pastor what Dontay was doing. The youth pastor became angry and walked toward Dontay. Others students are curious and watch Dontay's reading.

DISCUSS!

@ **Do you put any stock in psychics, palm readers, fortune tellers, or tarot card readers? Do you read your horoscope? Why?**

@ **Do you believe God gives everyone gifts—including psychics, palm readers, fortune tellers, or tarot card readers? Can someone have these "gifts" and still be a Christian? Why?**

@ **Does Satan give gifts?**

@ **Have you ever taken one of those tests that show up in your email to decide your future or forecast whom you will marry? If so, what did you learn from this?**

@ **Why do you think we are so obsessed with knowing what's going to happen?**

@ If we really had faith, wouldn't we ignore all the psychic and fortune-telling stuff? Why?

@ What is the effect of Dontay's reading on other group members? On his youth pastor?

Read:

Deuteronomy 18:9-14
Proverbs 19:21
Luke 12:16-20
James 4:13-16

@ When the youth pastor confronts Dontay, what should the youth pastor do? Why?

TAKE NOTES/MAKE NOTES

HOME FOR THE HOLIDAYS

Part of the divorce agreement was that Roberta would spend the holidays with her father. Every year, Roberta and her dad make the long drive to her grandparents. When there, Roberta must sit for two solid days and listen to her father argue with his grown siblings, hear her grandmother argue with her grandfather, and endure her aunt sitting and saying horrible things about her mother.

Roberta knows this rowtime will repeat itself as surely—and as often—as an old movie on the crummy local TV station.

It has been six years since the divorce and Roberta has not had a happy Christmas in all that time. Roberta is a senior this year. She turns 18 in November and will no longer be required to go with her father on holidays.

In a way she dreads being free of the obligation to make these trips. Now she will have to decide on her own to join these scenes, or endure additional grief for staying away.

Her mother insists that Roberta needs to spend time with her dad and his family. But Roberta cannot bear the idea of enduring another Christmas, hiding in the guest room at her grandmothers, while the rest of the family yells, screams and talks her mother down.

TAKE NOTES/MAKE NOTES

@ Does Roberta have the right to a merry Christmas? Explain.

@ If you were Roberta, and you did decide to keep celebrating the holidays with your dad, what would you do when the family started their fighting and gossiping again? Why?

@ Is Roberta ever going to change things at her father's house? Why?

@ Could you stand up for a family member who wasn't there to defend herself? Why?

@ Both her father and mother want Roberta to spend the holidays with her dad. Does honoring her father and mother mean "no matter what"? Why?

@ Should Roberta stand up for her mother against her father's relatives? Why?

@ If Roberta takes the trip, what is the upside for her of just quietly enduring all the fighting and criticism of her mother? The downside? What is the upside of confronting her adversarial relatives? The downside?

Ephesians 6:1-4
James 1:19
Psalm 27:10
2 Corinthians 6:11-13

@ Come up with a recipe for a merry Christmas for Roberta. What should she do? Say? What attitude should she maintain? Why?

TAKE NOTES/MAKE NOTES

REASON FOR THE SEASON

Zale is 14. Christmas is his favorite time of year. Ever since he was a kid he knew there was something magical about Christmas. He believed in Santa until long after most kids stopped. He has a favorite T-shirt that says, "I believe."

There is something about the holiday that lights something up inside Zale. His mother has told him he gets that from his grandmother who would keep the tree up all year long if she could. Zale and his grandmother are very close. Last year Zale's grandmother died on Christmas day. She died while getting the house ready for the family. When Zale and parents pulled into the driveway there was an ambulance in there.

It is a year later and Zale has no desire to celebrate whatsoever. He has asked his mother if he could stay home from the family gathering this year

@ Who was the person closest to you who died most recently? How did it affect you?

@ Have you ever celebrated a holiday that had a "hole" in it? Explain.

@ How long does it take to heal after the death of someone close to you? Why?

@ Could you celebrate Christmas in a prison cell? Alone in a foreign country? If there was no exchange of gifts? Why?

@ What is your favorite Christmas memory?

Philippians 2:5-11
Luke 6:38
Hebrews 10:24-25
John 14:1-4

@ If you were Zale, could you celebrate Christmas the way his grandmother would have wanted or would you take it quieter? Why?

WORSHIP

Derek grew up in a quiet little Presbyterian church. His family went every Sunday and he never missed Vacation Bible School. It is the only way that Derek has ever worshipped.

Derek has been dating Susan, a pretty girl from his high school choir. She invited him to her church on Sunday night. Derek has never worshipped any other time but Sunday morning at 10:30, but he accepts Susan's invite. It is just the beginning of him moving out of his comfort zone.

Susan's church is unlike anything he has ever seen. The worship is loud and people are dancing, jumping and waving their upraised hands as they sing. The preacher shouts his entire sermon, moving all around the platform, sweating profusely. At the sermon's end, everyone moves forward and the preacher lays hands on them and prays for them. Many pray loudly in tongues. Others fall down "under the power"—including Susan.

The service lasts two and a half hours. On their way out to the car Susan asks, "Wasn't that amazing? Didn't you feel God?"

DISCUSS:

@ How would you feel if you were Derek? Why?

    @ What's the most unusual thing you've ever seen in worship?

@ When something unusual happens in worship, should you write it off as wrong immediately, or take some time to carefully consider whether it is good or bad? Why?

@ What if Susan was invited to a full rite Catholic mass? Would it be any less awkward for her? Why?

@ Is there any kind of worship you consider wrong or bad? Explain.

@ Would you go out on a second date with someone who worshipped God in such a dramatically different way than you do? Why?

    @ Could you go out with someone who was part of a different religion? Could you date an atheist? Should you?

Read:

Matthew 6:5-8
Exodus 29:10-35
Hebrews 10:23-25
Galatians 3:28-29

@ How should Derek respond to Susan's question? Why?

    @ If you were Derek, would you go back to Susan's church again? Why?

PRIORITIES, COMMITMENT, CALLING

SCORE

Doreen is the highest scoring player on her school's volleyball team. Though the volleyball thing is important to Doreen, she is most excited about going into the Peace Corps after graduation.

Doreen's youth group is going to Haiti on a mission trip this year to help build a church. The youth minister has called a mandatory meeting for everyone planning to go on the trip. The meeting is scheduled for the same day as a volleyball game. Every player is allowed to miss only one game per season. Doreen must choose between the church meeting or the volleyball game.

Doreen chooses to attend the meeting. After the meeting, Doreen returns home and plays the messages on her machine. An angry friend is calling to let her know their team lost the game—in fact, it was a shut-out. Her friend closes the message with, "I hope you're happy."

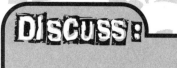

@ **What is loyalty?**

@ **Who are you most loyal to? Why?**

@ **Is church more important than school? Why?**

@ **Rank these in order of importance in your life...School, Church, God, Friends, Family. Explain.**

@ **Would you have gone to the meeting or the game? Why?**

@ **How would you react if you were on Doreen's team?**

Proverbs 17:17
Matthew 6:33
1 Tim 4:14

@ **What should Doreen do now?**

TO BURN OR NOT TO BURN?

Jonathan's church has a new youth minister. The new guy just started and most of the kids like him. He doesn't preach like their last youth minister. He likes discussions and leads some pretty fun games. A few kids left, but they were the ones who were never happy with anything the last youth minister did either.

Jonathan and Pedro were talking before the last meeting. Pedro handed Jonathan a freshly burned copy of a new CD. The new youth minister saw the copy and told Jonathan and Pedro that copying a CD was stealing. The youth pastor announces to the group that no one is to bring copied CD's into the church anymore. He also told them all that they weren't to copy CD's because it was against God's law.

Jonathan told him to lighten up because it was just a CD and everybody did it. A full-scale debate soon erupted. The entire youth group faced off against the new youth minister over the issue.

◉ **If everyone is doing something, does it make it okay? Why?**

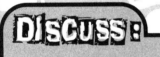

◉ **Is stealing always wrong? Is lying always wrong ("No, the dress doesn't make you look fat." "Yes, mom the meatloaf is good.")? Explain.**

◉ **Is it stealing to download and burn "shared" songs to a CD? Why?**

◉ **At a fast-food drive-through, if the worker gives you an extra sandwich you didn't pay for, would you give it back? Why?**

◉ **Your best friend works at the local movie theater and offers to get you and your date in free whenever they are on duty. How would you respond to this offer? Why?**

Luke 16:10
Jeremiah 17:10
Proverbs 21:2

◉ **What would you do if you were Jonathan?**

JOYFUL?

Joy isn't sure she likes the new minister at her church. The search committee interviewed over a dozen people and finally chose a woman who was about 50 and who looked like a schoolteacher.

She was sweet on the outside, but as soon as she got behind the pulpit, she used it to hammer on redemption, salvation and sanctification. These were topics the former minister barely ever mentioned, much less with a raised voice.

Last Sunday, as the congregation finished singing, "Joy to the World," the minister launched into a 45-minute attack on backsliding and emphasized that the one, true purpose of Christmas was redemption. Joy isn't sure she wants to go to this church anymore.

DISCUSS:

@ What is church-hopping? Why do people church-hop?

@ To see older members of a congregation who've been in one church for more than 50 years is unusual. Why?

@ What's the most important aspect or quality you look for in a church? Why?

@ Should preachers "tone down" their message in order to please people and keep them in the pews? Why?

@ Is the pulpit the place for hard preaching, encouraging people, or teaching people? Explain.

@ What kind of preaching do you prefe— fiery or gentle? Why?

@ Boil it down to a few words…what is a minister's job?

@ Should people too caught up in the "message" remember the "messenger"? Why? How?

Read:

Malachi 2:7
Hebrews 13:17-18
Titus 2:7-8

@ What would you do if you were Joy?

CONFIRMED

Camilla is a week away from confirmation. She's gone through the year-long course at her church and listened to everything her minister told her. This week he walked them through the entire confirmation service so they would know what it would be like.

Camilla reads the words and understands that next week she will say these beliefs as an oath before God. Camilla isn't sure she believes these things. She isn't sure she feels the words.

Her teacher constantly tells them they have to mean the promises when they say them. Camilla has no idea how to tell her teacher and her parents that she has decided not to be confirmed. Her parents have invited all their family and friends to the service. She just isn't sure she is ready.

 **Discuss:**

@ **Is faith more about believing or knowing? What difference might this make for Camilla as she sorts out her feelings? Why?**

@ **How far should you go to please your parents? Explain.**

@ **In light of the fact that all her family and friends have been invited to the service, should Camilla just go through with the service? Why?**

@ **Can you pray if you don't believe in God? What if you are just a little iffy on the details? Explain.**

@ **Which takes more maturity...to be confirmed and understand all that goes along with that or to not be confirmed when you aren't sure you mean it? Explain.**

 **Read:**

Mark 4:26-29
1 Timothy 3:5

@ **It is time to plan the service. What would you do if you were Camilla?**

CHEER

Last year, Byron got a job working in a fast food restaurant. This summer, his manager put him just a little bit less than full time for the whole ss, different groups use the parking lot for car washes.

Last Saturday, a group of high school cheerleaders were washing cars. Byron kept stealing glances out the drive thru window at the girls in short shorts and bathing suit tops as they splashed and sprayed each other with the hose. Byron wasn't aware he was staring as long as he was.

His manager saw him and gathered all the girls behind the counter together and had them stare at Byron. Finally she said, "Byron, take a picture; it will last longer." Byron was startled out of his daydream and the girls all laughed at him.

Since that day every girl in the place has treated him differently. They look at him like he's some sort of sex fiend or pervert. He mentioned this to the manager but she only said that it was his own fault for drooling over the cheerleaders in the parking lot.

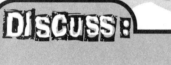

@ Was what the manager did fair? Why?

@ If it had been a guy's basketball team washing the cars shirtless and a girl employee was "looking," would that have been any different? Why?

@ Should guys be allowed to stare like Byron did because that's just something guys do? Why?

@ Was Byron doing anything wrong? When does looking or staring become wrong? Explain.

@ If a girl wears short shorts that have the word "CHEER" written across her backside…should she get mad if someone looks? If they stare? Why?

@ Are certain kinds of behavior excusable because someone is "a teenager"? Explain.

Psalm 139:23-24
Colossians 3:12-13

@ If you were Byron, what's your next move?

CROSSING THE LINE

Steve's youth minister saw in the paper that a new exhibit was being shown at the Center for Contemporary Art downtown. The exhibit was called "CROSS" and all the artwork displayed would feature a cross or a crucifix in some manner.

The youth minister organized a quick trip on a Saturday and 15 teenagers rode to the Center with him to see the exhibit. As Steve wandered around, he saw a photograph that he thought was quite beautiful. It was a close up shot of Jesus on a cross. The photo seemed to have been shot through a gold filter. It was his favorite part of the exhibit and he told the rest of the group about it.

On the way home, Steve's youth minister told him that the piece he admired so much was one where the artist had taken a crucifix, put it into a jar of his own urine and then snapped the photograph.

@ Was this a good idea for a youth group trip? Why?

@ Where is your own personal line of "what is appropriate?" Why?

@ Can art be blasphemous? Can blasphemy be art? Why?

@ What is art?

@ How might Steve's feelings about the golden crucifix have changed in light of the urine "revelation"? What if Steve had never known the photo's origin?

@ Are there some things that should just not be done with the image of Christ? Why?

@ What would happen if they used Jesus to sell shoes? Cars? Sunday School Curriculum?

@ What does Christ's sacrifice on the cross mean to you? Why?

1 Corinthians 1:26
Romans 8:28

@ What are Steve's options?

DISTURBING VISUALS, FREEDOM OF EXPRESSION, RESPECTING GOD

REFERENCES

Dinah and Molly have been best friends for a long time. Dinah got a job at a supermarket as a cashier for the summer. Molly needed a job too, so Dinah pulled some strings and got her friend an interview. When the manager came to Dinah and asked about Molly, Dinah gave her a good reference and Molly was hired.

Soon things went sour. Molly was always late, her cash drawer seldom totaled up correctly and several customers went to the manager to complain about Molly's attitude. The manager told Dinah that he was disappointed in her because of her recommendation.

Molly was soon fired and Dinah could tell Molly thought it was somehow her fault. Dinah has also noticed that the manager has slowly been cutting Dinah's hours and bringing a new girl in to work her shifts.

DISCUSS:

@ Would you do anything for a friend, even if you knew it was a bad idea? Why?

@ How hard would it be to be your best friend's boss? Employee? Why?

@ Do certain "rules of friendship" need to be suspended in certain situations? Explain.

@ Which "rules of friendship" would need to be suspended for Dinah and Molly's situation to work out? Why?

@ If a friend couldn't handle the pressure, would you recommend that person for the job?

@ If a friend approached you for a job reference and you knew they would not do a good job, would you still give them a reference? Why?

@ Should your first loyalty be to your friend or the one who signs your paycheck? Why?

@ Who's right in this situation? Why?

Romans 12:3
Proverbs 17:17; 27:6; 27:10; 27:17

◎ How can Dinah get things back together with Molly?
With her employer?

◎ What can Dinah learn from this? Explain.

TAKE NOTES/MAKE NOTES

EYE OF THE BEHOLDER

Melinda and a few of her friends have noticed lately that the boys in their school think it's cool to wear T-shirts from a local chain of restaurants who's claim to fame is scantily clad waitresses.

The T-shirts feature two giant eyeballs on the chest. When the waitresses wear these shirts, the eyeballs look as though they are popping out.

"Eyes popping out…exactly what happens to all the guys!" Melinda told her friends.

More and more at the school, guys are wearing the shirts as a status symbol and Melinda has had enough. Melinda designs a T-shirt with the name of a fictitious restaurant called "Tusks." The T-shirt design features an elephant whose trunk is as suggestive of a guy as the eyes are meant to be nasty cartoons of girls' features.

Melinda made several of these shirts and gave them to her friends. Soon others want them, so she has to make more.

Yesterday Melinda was called to the principal's office who told her enough was enough. She wasn't to wear or give away the "Tusks" shirts on school property. When Melinda pointed out the T-shirts the boys were wearing, the principal said that was different, because their T-shirts depicted a real restaurant.

TAKE NOTES/MAKE NOTES

🌀 Give me a working definition of the word "appropriate." How important is it for Christians to stay well within the bounds of appropriate? Why?

🌀 What does the old phrase mean that goes, "What's good for the goose is good for the gander?" Is it true? If so, does it apply here? Why?

🌀 Why do certain things get labeled as being "cool"? What makes something "cool"? Explain.

🌀 Have you ever seen a school that had a uniform policy? Does this help cut down on situations like this? How? Why?

(NOTE: While this discussion could easily become one about "Why guys do that…" or "Why girls do this…," try to keep the group focused on Melinda's situation. Then allow it to go where it goes.)

Matthew 7:9
Ecclesiastes 9:11

🌀 If you were Melinda, could you put the shirt on for school the next day? What would your other options be?

TAKE NOTES/MAKE NOTES

MY WAY

Bill is sitting in study hall, reading. That is it. He's not being disruptive. He's not talking or passing notes. He is simply reading.

The book he has chosen to read is, *My Way or the Highway*. It's written by Zack Langer, a controversial "shock jock" who has a nationally broadcast, morning radio show. He's been called racist, sexist and a "bad influence on America's youth."

The book is chapter after chapter of ranting and raving about all Zack Langer thinks is wrong with the world. His outrageous views on pornography, "dirty words," and sex are each given a chapter in his book.

Langer has been the subject of many TV news and magazine aritcles. Virtually everyone in the country knows this man and his views.

In the middle of study hall, Mrs. Jefferson asks Bill to give her the book. She tells him that it violates the school's obscenity policy and that his mother or father will have to come in to get the book back for him.

Bill thinks Mrs. Jefferson is taking the book only because of Zack Langer's politics and his views on women. He doesn't think he's doing anything wrong by reading the book.

TAKE NOTES/MAKE NOTES

Discuss:

@ What do you think of Bill's decision to read the Zack Langer book?

@ What's the risk of reading such a book? Benefits? Explain.

@ Why do schools make rules about what you can and can't bring or wear to school? As long as it's not hurting anybody…what's the harm?

@ If a culture has deemed certain words to be unacceptable, why do some people want to say them over and over? And if a society has decided that certain things cannot be said or done…shouldn't they be punished when done? Why?

@ Would you let little kids watch an R rated movie? Why or why not?

@ We cannot control those who have authority over us, but what can we control? Explain.

@ How come it seems like what is fun isn't "good" and what is "good" is boring?

Read:

Romans 13:1-7
James 4:4-10

@ How should Bill respond to Mrs. Jefferson's accusation? Why?

TAKE NOTES/MAKE NOTES

SNAPSHOT

Chuck and Patrick were with the church youth group on the annual trip to Mystic Mountain, an amusement park that features more rides and coasters than any other park in the state. They've been riding all the rides and are having a blast.

Suddenly they spot Betty Bumble, the "girlfriend" of the park's mascot Bucky. Betty is a seven-foot Dinosaur in a neon pink dress. Chuck tells Patrick he wants his picture taken with Betty Bumble.

Chuck stands in the "meet and greet" line with a bunch of kids who are about half his size. When it's his turn, Chuck stands next to Betty and Patrick takes out his disposable camera.

Just before the picture is snapped, Chuck reaches up and grabs one of Betty's breasts. Chuck is pretty sure it was a guy in the suit because "Betty" belts him in the head, knocking him to the ground.

Within two minutes, park security has Chuck and Patrick surrounded and promptly escort them to the park exit. It is about five more hours until they have to meet up with the group to go home.

@ Was this funny? Why?

@ Would it have been fun had it not been done in front of little kids? Why?

@ Have you ever heard the phase "Stupid is as stupid does"? Is it true? Give an example.

@ Would you say or do anything if you were the one kicked out? Why?

@ Have you ever been asked to leave an amusement park, restaurant, a mall, or any other place of business? Explain.

It's cool to have fun, but when does it get to the point where our representation of Christ is adversely affected by our fun? Explain and give an example.

Can you push a joke too far? Explain.

Genesis 4:6
1 Peter 2:8
Ecclesiastes 3:1-8

What would you do if you were Chuck?

What would you do if you were Patrick?

TAKE NOTES/MAKE NOTES

PARTY ON

Sharon's best friend, Donna, is a freshman at Carson State University. Sharon is a high school senior and plans to go to Carson next year. She's visited Donna on campus several times, typically staying through the weekend.

Sharon's parents think she's going to get to know the campus and to sit in on some classes. Though Sharon does sit in on a class or two each trip, the primary focus of her trips is really the weekend partying.

At every frat party, Sharon ends up drunk out of her mind and wakes up with a different guy in bed with her. Sharon has had sex with several college guys over the last two months.

Now Sharon sits in a doctor's office. She had to get a physical to go on a summer trip overseas. The doctor tells her that blood tests showed she is HIV positive.

DISCUSS:

@ **Other than the obvious, what would be the first thing you would do? Why?**

@ **How should Sharon tell her parents? How do you think they will respond? Why?**

@ **How should Sharon inform the guys she's had sex with that they may be HIV positive? Explain.**

@ **Should Sharon continue with her plans and go to Carson State in the Fall or not? Why?**

@ **Is HIV a judgment from God on sinners? Explain.**

@ **Is it fair for anyone to get HIV? Why?**

@ **Is what happened to Sharon fair? Explain.**

ALCOHOL/ DRINKING, PARTYING, SEX

@ Do we get what we deserve in life? When is that a good thing? When is that a bad thing? Explain.

@ If you were Sharon's friend what would be the best way to share Christ with her? Explain.

 Read:

Proverbs 5:1-23
Psalm 51:
Isaiah 54:4-8
John 16:21

@ What should Sharon do?

TAKE NOTES/MAKE NOTES

FOR THE GLORY

Bart, Anthony and Dennis are all in the eleventh grade. They all like to meet at a downtown plaza on Saturdays. They hang out, throw a Frisbee, and occasionally get into trouble, but nothing too serious.

They've been friends for years and have been going to the plaza all their lives. The plaza seems to attract "street preachers," as Bart calls them. Loud, shouting Christians who stand near the fountain, wave their Bibles, and tell whatever crowd appears about the "good news" of Jesus Christ.

The trio has often listened to the street preachers, even razzing them occasionally, from the crowd. Anthony is particularly unmoved by their message. His mother used to drag him to church services where preachers would scream and yell and tell him why he was going to hell. To him, it's a big joke.

Today "Brother Ted" and "Sister Kelly" are at the fountain and are loudly "sharing" God's message with the crowd. Anthony leans over to Bart and says "I'll give you five bucks if you go up there and ask sister Kelly if she wants to make out." Bart stifles a chuckle and moves forward.

On page two of the Sunday paper is a photo taken at the plaza, of Sister Kelly hitting a young man (Bart) with her Bible.

TAKE NOTES/MAKE NOTES

Was Bart's joke just "boys will be boys" or did he go too far? Why?

Was Sister Kelly's action Christian or hypocritical? Why?

How would you react if you were Bart's parents and saw the picture of your son being hit by a street preacher? Why?

Do you give more respect to preachers than other people, just because they are preachers? Explain.

Is street preaching an effective way to share faith? Why?

How far should one go to share their faith? Why?

Jesus used to point out the hypocrisy of the Pharisees, is this situation any different?

What if Bart had said something ruder to Sister Kelly? Do degrees of rudeness make a real difference?

John 7:16-18
Matthew 23:7

Any chance Bart apologized to Sister Kelly afterwards? Why?

What should he do?

TAKE NOTES/MAKE NOTES

APPEARANCES

Ben is in the tenth grade and is a big, burly guy. He was allowed to join the varsity football team when he was in the ninth grade because of his size. At 16, he towered over most of his teachers and outweighed the next biggest player by twenty-five pounds. Ben's coach told his parents that offers would soon be coming from colleges, as Ben got a little older.

Ben was a decent student. Not the best, but not the worst. He worked his butt off most of the time and held a three point zero average. A few weeks ago, Mrs. Cole, Ben's English teacher, asked him if he would read aloud from the literature textbook. It was a poem by Emily Dickinson. He read the poem. A few of the guys snickered and Mrs. Cole said, "Thank you, Ben. That was very nice."

Ben knew he was changed forever. For the first time ever, he understood poetry. He read all of the poems in the book that night at home. The next day Mrs. Cole asked him if someone had helped him with his home-work. When he assured her he had not received help, she marveled at his remarkable insights on the poems.

That night Ben snuck into his sister's room and "borrowed" a few of her poetry books. He was hooked. He began sneaking books of poetry from school and read-ing them in his room at night. His sister caught him tak-ing her books and threatened to tell all his friends. Ben's biggest fear is being labeled a poetry lover or a wimp.

DISCUSS:

⚉ How important is it for you to keep up "appear-ances"? Why?

⚉ Think about the students in your school. How important is it for them to keep up "appearances"? Why?

⚉ When you find your "passion" (what deeply satisfies you, captivates you, something you are skilled in, or something that pleases you) is it important to nurture it? Why? What happens if you deny your passion?

⚉ Have you ever known someone who gave up on his or her dream a long time ago? Why did they give up?

🌀 What is a "calling"?

🌀 If God puts a "calling" on you, must you follow it? Why? What happens if you turn away from it?

🌀 What would you do if everything you always wanted to be suddenly became the opposite of who you knew that you were in your heart?

🌀 How important is it to survive high school with one's "rep" intact? Explain.

🌀 If the "real you" is someone you know will be rejected or not be respected, would you play along with the crowd and be someone they will love and respect—then be your true self later? Why?

 Read:

1 Corinthians 12:4-6
Luke 8:4-8

🌀 What would you do if you were Ben? Go on boldly...or quietly?

TAKE NOTES/MAKE NOTES

SIDES

Dwight's sister Kelly is openly gay. She and her partner, Maggie, have come to the house several times since their "union ceremony." To Dwight's family, it is not even an issue that gets discussed.

The city where Dwight lives is currently considering an amendment to the city charter that would prohibit employers and landlords from denying work and housing to a person, based on their sexual orientation. Dwight's government teacher decides to hold one of his famous impromptu debates.

"All those in favor of the amendment, move to the left side of the room," the teacher said, "all those opposed to the amendment, stand on the right side of the room."

Dwight took only a second to get his books together, but when he looks up, he sees that 90 percent of the class is on the right side of the room. There are three people on the left.

His classmates know Dwight is a Christian. A number of them, standing on the right side, go to the large youth group he attends. That youth group teaches that homosexual activity is a sin. Dwight isn't sure he believes that—but he does feel that people should not be denied housing and job opportunities.

Dwight is still sitting in the middle of the room when the teacher says, "Well Dwight, what's it going to be?"

@ **What does the Bible say about all the issues presented here?**

@ **What happens when you have an opinion not held by the majority? Explain.**

@ **If Dwight stands up with those who are in favor of the amendment, what might happen in his relationships with the youth group members who are all against it? Why?**

@ **Should Dwight's relationships with other youth group members be negatively affected by his difference of belief on this issue? Why?**

@ If it was a matter of your own well-being (mentally or physically), would you stand with the majority, even if you didn't agree with them? Why?

@ Would you stand against the majority if it meant you stood for what you really believe, even if you might lose friends? Why?

@ Would you stand up for a belief, even if it meant you might go to jail? Be beaten? Be killed? Why?

@ For what beliefs would you take the strongest, bravest stand? Why?

Read:

Matthew 5:33-37
1 Peter 3:15-16

@ What would you do if you were Dwight?

TAKE NOTES/MAKE NOTES

HELP ME

The most gorgeous girl in Robert's American History Class has sat across from him for an entire year without saying anything more than "hello" to him.

This morning, before the mid-term, she started openly flirting with him. She called him by his name, looked fully into his eyes as she smiled at him and touched his shoulder when she talked.

Robert can't help but think that all the times he has been nice to her, and in some blind way all the time and intense attention he has silently paid, is bearing fruit.

During the exam, she drums lightly on her desk with her red fingernails to get his attention. He looks over and she points to the first question on her paper. It is blank. She gestures as if to say, "Help me." Then she smiles one of her killer smiles at him again.

Her smile renders him powerless. Though Robert feels a little turn-off that she seems to be playing him, he is enjoying the attention and thinking about the possibilities.

And he is thinking less and less about the test, and pride in his results

TAKE NOTES/MAKE NOTES

DISCUSS:

⊚ If Robert gives this gorgeous girl the answers, is he a master romantic strategist, or just a guy with low self esteem? Explain.

⊚ In the big scheme of things, can a little cheating really be such a bad thing? It's just a little help…what's the harm? Explain.

⊚ Have you ever had someone play you like this? How? Why?

⊚ Are you close to someone who plays or uses others? If so, describe what that's like.

⊚ Who is someone you know who doesn't play or use others, who is loving and treats others with respect? Tell about that person.

⊚ Have you ever played someone to get something you wanted? How? Why?

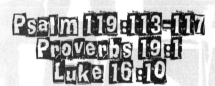
Psalm 119:113-117
Proverbs 19:1
Luke 16:10

⊚ Would you help the girl? Why?

TAKE NOTES/MAKE NOTES

GUESS WHO'S COMING TO DINNER?

Corey and three of his friends are sitting in a crowded restaurant. Their waitress has been kind, but in a hurry. The place is chaotic, full of people and there is a long line waiting to get in.

The friends are all complaining about how tight money is for them right now. They talk about all the movies they want to see. And they start sharing stories of crazy, mischievous things they've all done in the past.

Corey has no stories to tell. He really doesn't do sneaky or mischievous things. His friends let him know they'd love to see that side of him.

One of Corey's friends suggests that with the crowd the way it is, they could easily sneak out without paying. Then they could use the money they save to see a movie and buy popcorn and refreshments as well.

The group agrees, but it will only work if they all do it. One friend realizes Corey hasn't said he'll walk out with them.

"Well Cor, what's it gonna be? You need to get a little crazy in your life." They all look at Corey.

TAKE NOTES/MAKE NOTES

DISCUSS:

@ Is sneaking out of the restaurant just an innocent prank, or something worse? Why?

@ If they follow through on sneaking out, what will be the effect on the waitress? The restaurant? Other students who dine in groups there? Will they ever be able to eat there again? Why?

@ Have you ever stolen or shoplifted even something little? A can of soda pop? A pen? Why?

@ Does the size of the item you take matter? Why?

@ Should Corey sneak out just to keep from getting in trouble with his friends? Why?

@ Imagine you sneak out and the next day you meet your waitress on the street. What would you say?

 Read:

Proverbs 4:10-16
1 Timothy 6:11

@ What would you do if you were Corey?

TAKE NOTES/MAKE NOTES

SURFACING

Ryan has been grounded for two months. He took the car without permission and went riding around with his friends. For the last sixty days, he has been allowed to go only to school, work and church.

Ryan's grounding will be up on Friday night and two of his friends plan to take him out to celebrate. Ryan is scheduled to work the whole weekend. He calls in sick on Friday and goes out with his friends.

On Saturday Ryan's boss asks, "So, how are you feeling?" Ryan wonders if his boss knows he wasn't really sick.

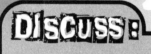 **DISCUSS:**

@ **Is lying to get a sick day from work really a big deal? Why?**

@ **Is it possible for a person to be totally honest all the time? Why?**

@ **Is there ever a time when you have to lie? When? Why?**

@ **Is it ever okay to lie—like to tell a "white" lie? When? Why?**

@ **Do you think Ryan learned anything from his grounding? Why?**

@ **Would you describe Ryan as responsible? Why?**

@ **Have you ever had someone look you in the face and lie through their teeth? Did you know then that they were lying? How did it make you feel?**

@ **How important is it to you that your closest friends are honest with you? Why?**

 **Read:**   **Proverbs 12:17-22**

@ **What would you do if you were Ryan?**

GUESS WHO'S COMING TO DINNER PART 2

Corey is in a crowded restaurant with 11 of his friends. They have had a great time, though they've been a little loud.

The waitress has been rushing back and forth between their group and several other tables. The meal was good, on time, and the waitress probably put up with more than she had too. Everyone gets their check and starts to leave.

Corey notices that no one leaves a tip. He mentions this and most of the others have some excuse about why they aren't leaving any money. Corey has enough money to cover his meal, a tip and a little extra, but not much.

@ **Why do we leave tips?**

@ **Why does it seem like we're losing money when we leave a tip?**

@ **Have you or someone you know ever waited tables? If so, talk about what it's like and what tips mean to the waiter or waitress. If not, what do you think would be the toughest part of being a waiter or waitress?**

@ **Is it fair for the waiter or waitress if we leave no tip? Why? What if service was not better than average, should you still tip? Why?**

@ **Who do you guess are the best tippers? Why?**

@ **Have you ever left more than 15 percent as a tip? Why?**

@ **What would you say to your friends who were walking away without leaving a tip?**

@ **Tell about the best service you ever received in a restaurant and why you felt the service was so good.**

 **Ephesians 4:23-24
Matthew 22:39**

@ **What would you do if you were Corey?**

NOT MY GIRL

Jackie is sitting at her dinner table with her family. Her younger sister mentions that the school is going to be creating a day-care center for teenagers with babies.

Jackie's father goes off on a long tirade about the failure of the education system and how girls used to be shipped off to live with relatives if that happened which was rare. It was something to be ashamed of not shown off.

Jackie's father rants for five minutes and then turns to Jackie and says, "At least I'll never have to worry about my girls getting pregnant." He begins eating again.

Jackie is two months pregnant.

TAKE NOTES/MAKE NOTES

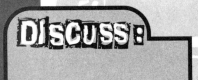

@ Do you think high school should provide day-care for babies of teenagers? Why?

@ Should school rest rooms have vending machines that distribute condoms or other forms of birth control? Why?

@ If a youth group member becomes pregnant, how should the youth group respond: throw her a shower, kick her out, do something else? Why?

@ What do you think Jackie's dad's reaction is going to be when he learns his daughter is pregnant? Would he send her away? Why?

@ Put yourself in the dad's place. Suppose Jackie blurted out that she was pregnant right there at the table. What would he say or do? What would you say or do? Why?

James 4:13-17
1 Peter 1:3-6
Hebrews 12:1-17

@ What would you do if you were Jackie?

TAKE NOTES/MAKE NOTES

PREGNANCY, LOVE, GRACE

TRUTH JUSTICE AND THE AMERICAN WAY

Jason has landed a great, but low-paying Job. He works at a comic book store. As much as he likes the job, he's not making much money after paying taxes, gas and insurance. Jason has tried to find something with higher pay, but there isn't anything out there and he doesn't want to flip burgers.

One of his friends at school says that to make some quick money, he should mark down a few of the collectible comics, sell them to a buddy, then take them across town to another shop and sell them for a sweet profit. Jason's friend tells him it would just be temporary until he gets another job.

His friend tells him, "If you really feel bad about it, you can always give the money back someday. But hey, just think of all the money they make off what you sell…and how little you get paid. You're just getting back what you're owed."

TAKE NOTES/MAKE NOTES

© If Jason did this, would he simply be getting what he is "owed"? Explain your reasoning.

© Why do most people feel they are "owed" more than what they currently make? Are they right? Why?

© Would this truly be a victimless crime? Why?

© What if Jason worked at a jewelry store, and this was a situation about diamonds valued in thousands of dollars—is it still a victimless crime? Explain.

© What are some other options for Jason to get some extra cash?

Proverbs 16:8; 18:9
1 Timothy 6:4-8

© What would you do if you were Jason? Why?

© What would you do if you were Jason and got caught?

© What would you do if you were the comic shop owner?

TAKE NOTES/MAKE NOTES

SPIKE

Tory and Janelle have been friends for a long time. They are both on the varsity volleyball team. It's early in the year and the coach is talking about having to cut one player.

Tory and Janelle decide they will team up and help each other out. Neither of them likes Joanna very much. She never hangs out with the rest of the team and she always wears shoes that Tory and Janelle think are stupid. For the good of the team, they decide to make sure Joanna is off the team.

They strategize that they can set each other up to score while at the same time making Joanna look bad. They execute their plan perfectly.

At the end of practice, the coach walks into the locker room and tells Joanna to meet him in his office. After a few minutes, Joanna leaves slowly and Tory and Janelle high five each other.

@ Aren't sports a matter of "survival of the fittest"? If so, isn't Tory and Janelle's plan fair? Explain.

@ What would you be willing to do for the "greater good" of the team? Why?

@ The Bible says that "trials" build character, so shouldn't Joanna be grateful for what happened? Why?

@ Have you ever had someone "gang up" on you unfairly? Tell us about it.

@ Why do you think people do this kind of thing?

@ What would you do if you were Joanna and you did not know what Tory and Janelle did? What if you found out what Tory and Janelle did?

What would you do if you were on the team and found out what Tory and Janelle did? Why?

Would it matter if you might be the one who was cut if you told?

 **Read:** **Romans 12:8-10 Luke 10:25-37**

If someone knew about Tory and Janelle's plan, what should they do?

TAKE NOTES/MAKE NOTES

JESUS WHO?

Doreen and Barb go to the same school, they even share the same homeroom. Doreen is on the girl's swim team and is chairwoman of the prom committee. She is very popular. Guys want to date her. Girls want to hang out with her.

Barb is none of these. Doreen and Barb also go to the same church. In church on Sundays, Doreen is happy to talk with Barb. They sit together at youth group meetings and ride together to youth activities. But Doreen is trying to keep her school life separate from her church life. She won't even acknowledge Barb in the hallway when she is with her friends. She walks right past Barb as if she isn't there.

Barb has overheard Doreen saying "High school is a matter of survival and friendship with the right people is essential."

Apparently, Barb doesn't quite fit that "right people" profile.

TAKE NOTES/MAKE NOTES

@ Describe the kind of person Doreen might consider to be the "right" people to hang around. Explain.

@ Is Doreen right about high school being a matter of survival? That friendship with the right people is essential? Why?

@ How do these ideas match with what you know of Christianity? Why?

@ Tell us about someone you know who lives Christ "loudly" in school? What do other people think of that Christian? Why?

@ Jesus talked about being rejected for his sake. Has this ever happened to you? Tell us about it.

@ Do you know anyone like Doreen? What kinds of things do they do to "transform" to the school setting? How do you feel toward them? Why?

@ Is there a different "you" that you put on when you go to school? Why?

 **Philippians 2:1-11
James 2:1-13
John 3:13-18**

@ What would you do if you were Barb?

@ What would you do it you were Doreen's youth minister and she told you the importance of hanging with the right people? Why?

TAKE NOTES/MAKE NOTES

PROMISES, PROMISES

Keith was confirmed just two weeks ago. In front of God, friends and family, he stood up and made a vow that he would live his life a certain way. Now he stands in the middle of a loud party, celebrating the imminent demise of the current school year.

One of his friends is a graduating senior whose name he can't remember (Sarah? Selena? Susie?). Keith's parent's think he is at his friend Nick's house. He's had had four beers. He cussed out a freshman earlier and everyone thought he was funny. Now standing in the bedroom of the graduating senior, he is slowly unbuttoning her shirt.

Looking over her shoulder, he sees himself in the mirror. In a corner of the mirror, wedged under the frame, is the girl's confirmation certificate. It is just like his confirmation certificate (and her name is Serena).

In a matter of hours, Keith has violated every promise he made to God just two weeks ago.

TAKE NOTES/MAKE NOTES

DISCUSS:

@ Are church and "real life" two separate things? Explain.

@ Does anyone really keep their confirmation promises to God? If they do, what does that mean? If they don't, does that really change anything? Why?

@ What is the point of making promises to God if no one can keep them?

@ When has standing strong on a commitment you made kept you from falling into temptation?

@ What does it take to maintain a strong commitment to God?

@ Is Christianity a lot to expect from anyone? Is it harder for some than others? Why?

@ What would you say to the girl, if you were Keith, right at that moment? Why?

Read:

Proverbs 30:32
Matthew 26:36-41
1 Corinthians 13:16
Psalm 130

@ What should Keith decide and do? Why?

TAKE NOTES/MAKE NOTES

HALLIE'S FRIEND

Hallie has been taking a serious self-inventory lately and she isn't all that thrilled with what she is seeing inside. What she sees is a shallow, self-centered, uncaring, rude person. She is determined to change her life and be a better person. She wants to be more like Jesus.

Hallie's youth minister taught a lesson last Sunday about how Jesus reached out and befriended the friendless. It really struck a chord with Hallie. She is going to be kinder, more caring and more accepting of others.

Monday morning, Hallie hiked up her courage and, ignoring what her friends might think, asked if she could sit at the table with a younger girl who always seemed to eat alone. Ever since, the younger girl thinks they are best friends. She follows Hallie around and calls her house every night. Today, Hallie got to school to find a "Best Friend" greeting card shoved into the vent of her locker.

"This is too much," Hallie said, "Jesus did not have to deal with this."

DISCUSS:

@ **Ever had a friend who was a little too clingy? How did you handle it? Why?**

@ **If we truly love people, should their clinginess, or any other shortcoming, bother us or cause us to stop loving them? Why?**

@ **Did Jesus have to "deal with this?" What did he do?**

@ **Is it possible to be "too nice"? Explain.**

@ **Is it possible for someone to take advantage of your niceness? If you are truly being nice should it bother you if someone does take advantage of you? Why?**

FRIENDLINESS, CHRISTLIKENESS, SELF-SACRIFICE

How can you let someone down without hurting his or her feelings?

Can you think of someone that you used to annoy the heck out of? What happened?

Read:

Matthew 5:24-34
1 Corinthians 9:19-23
James 2:1-4
Philippians 4:9

What would you do if you were Hallie?

What would you do if you were the girl with whom Hallie had lunch?

TAKE NOTES/MAKE NOTES

IS THIS IT?

At the end of the rally, Mark went forward with about fifteen other teenagers and gave his life to Jesus. He felt wonderful. The others in the group all slapped him on the back and hugged him. They all seemed genuinely happy for him.

What bothers Mark now is that he doesn't know any more than he did. All the answers to his faith questions that he thought would come more easily to him now have just not shown up. His friends in the group just sort of roll their eyes when Mark wants to have a serious discussion about God's plan and Jesus' teachings. They tell him to go talk with Rev. Barber, the youth pastor.

Mark feels Rev. Barber is getting tired of his questions. In truth, Rev. Barber doesn't like being sidelined by Mark and his questions on youth service nights when so many other kids are vying for his attention. Rev. Barber likes to focus on fun activities like water balloon fights and planning mission trips—his passion.

Mark is starting to feel like he did the "give-yourself-to-Jesus" thing wrong. How come nobody else is asking the same things that he is? Why is there no one who seems interested in going deeper or supporting him in going deeper?

TAKE NOTES/MAKE NOTES

- Is it possible to get the "give-yourself-to-Jesus" thing wrong? Why?

- In reality, how much should God and Jesus be part of a church youth group? Is it all supposed to de deep spiritual discussions and seriousness? Why?

- Should ministers ever get tired of doing one-on-one counseling with people in regard to their faith, or talking about God? Why?

- What are your perceptions of what happens after you give your life to Christ? Why?

- Does life get easier and happier after you give your life to Christ or harder and more serious? Why?

- What do you think the disciple's perception was on what happens after you commit to Christ? Explain.

John 1:35-42
Psalm 85
Jeremiah 29:13

- What would you do if you were Mark?

TAKE NOTES/MAKE NOTES

CORNERS

Jill has been swamped lately. The worst part is that she isn't swamped with fun things. It's all school, work, softball, plus she volunteered to help out at her church and has had to go to Sunday School helper training. She hasn't been dating anyone because she's been so loaded down with everything else. She can't figure out what to cut out from her life.

Her English teacher reminds the class that tomorrow is the day the book reports are due. Jill has not even begun to read the book. She is also scheduled to work tonight.

She knows she can find information about the book online. She also knows her sister did a report on the same book two years ago and got an "A." A few hours of copying and she can have a report without ever having opened the book.

Jill tells herself this is just a matter of cutting corners to save time. What choice does she have? Besides, it's not like she's been running around, wasting time, going to the mall and having fun with friends—she's been working constantly. She deserves a break.

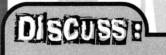

DISCUSS:

@ Did Jill have choices at one time to stay out of this mess? What were those choices? How could she have chosen differently? Explain.

@ Is there any difference between big lies and little lies? Explain.

@ If the definition of integrity is: "The kind of person you are when no one else is looking, " how much integrity does Jill have? Explain.

@ How much integrity do you have? Why?

@ Do you typically make the right decision no matter how difficult it makes your life, no matter what it costs, no matter how hard? Why?

◉ Are your feelings and taking "the easy way out" more of your guide when making tough decisions or pleasing God? Why?

◉ Does living Jill's way make life harder or make life easier? Why? Does it matter? Why?

 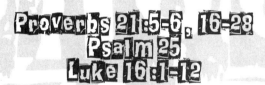

Proverbs 21:5-6, 16-28
Psalm 25
Luke 16:1-12

◉ What would you do if you were Jill?

TAKE NOTES/MAKE NOTES

FESSING UP

Kylie usually doesn't drink. It was a Friday night. The football game was over and a whole group of kids were in a parking lot, eating fast food and having a few beers. No one was drunk. There wasn't even that much beer there. Kylie is handed a beer can and she takes a long drink.

Just then, she spotted Mrs. Halliburton driving by. Mrs. Halliburton is also known as "Gossiping Gerty" in her church. It doesn't matter that everybody knows her tendency to exaggerate and sometimes lie—everybody listens to what she says.

Kylie knows that by the time she gets home "Gerty" will have already called her parents and told them that she was on a drunken rampage, driving drunk or having sex in the parking lot. Her parents will want to know where she was and what she was doing.

DISCUSS:

@ **Have you ever gossiped? Exaggerated? Expanded the truth? Why?**

@ **Should someone in the church confront Gerty about her gossiping? Why?**

@ **In situations like this one, is it ever better to just keep your mouth shut and take your chances? Why?**

@ **Tell us about a time when you were gossiped about. How did it affect you? Afterwards, did you tend to gossip less? Why?**

@ **Who does gossip hurt? Why?**

Read:

James 4:17
Isaiah 33:15-16
Proverbs 11:1-3

@ **What should Kylie do? Should she say something to her parents before they say something to her? Why?**

LIKE A PRAYER

Tara is incredibly happy. Jared, the hot guy she's been hoping would ask her out, just did. It's just a Saturday morning thing, bagels and coffee, but she thinks it's a great first date.

He picks her up and they have a sort of nervous conversation while they drive, but eventually it becomes comfortable and they are both enjoying themselves. They find a table in the crowded café.

As Tara reaches for the knife to spread cream cheese on her bagel, Jared takes her hand and begins to say grace. He prays for her. He prays for the people who made the bagel. He thanks God for the wonderful day.

Tara is looking around. Everyone seems to be looking at her. Jared says "Amen", lets go of her hand and begins to eat his own bagel, with no explanation.

@ **Why do you think Tara was affected as she was? Explain.**

@ **Could Jared have handled this a little differently? How? Should he have handled this differently? Why?**

@ **Are you a spiritual extrovert or a spiritual introvert? Why? Is it wrong to be spiritually introverted? Why?**

@ **Do you pray in public places, for any reason? Why? If not, have you ever been with someone who did? Describe how the experience affected you.**

@ **Are you a good Christian if pray a "blessing" before each meal? A bad Christian if you don't? Why? What would happen if you forgot to ask a blessing over your food?**

@ **Some believed in saying a meal "blessing" after the meal. Others believe you should pray before a meal. Which one of these views is right? Why?**

@ **Why do you think prayer in public can make some people uncomfortable?**

@ **Is there ever a wrong time or place to pray? Why?**

Matthew 6:1, 5-15
Romans 8: 21-26
Luke 11:1-13
Philippians 4:4-7

@ **What would you do if you were Tara?**

@ **What would you do if you were Jared and Tara asked you not to do that anymore?**

OLD-FASHIONED

Mr. Harrison is a sweet old guy. He is the supervisor at the market where Sherri works. Mr. Harrison is "old fashioned," as he says. "Behind the times" is how Allison, Sherri's co-worker describes him.

Mr. Harrison refuses to let the girls lift heavy boxes or climb ladders and always makes sure someone opens the door for them because they are "ladies." Sherri thinks he is being sweet and respectful.

Allison sees it totally differently. She believes Mr. Harrison considers them weak and incapable of doing the job. To back up her point she shares her perception that Mr. Harrison is giving more hours to guy employees because he believes girls can't do the work.

Sherri is content with the way things are and even appreciates that Mr. Harrison is showing some of the guys what it is to be a gentleman. But she does wonder if Allison is right about the guys getting more hours. That would be a big issue for her. Allison says she is going to report Mr. Harrison to the owners for discrimination.

TAKE NOTES/MAKE NOTES

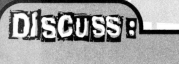

DISCUSS:

How do Allison and Sherri see Mr. Harrison so differently? Why?

Do you agree more with Allison or Sherri's view of Mr. Harrison? Why?

Are there some people who seem to enjoy playing the "victim"? Explain.

Is Mr. Harrison doing anything wrong? Why?

Isn't Mr. Harrison allowed to his run his business the way he sees fit? Explain.

Are you ever suspicious of the kindness of others? Why?

Should Sherri say something to Mr. Harrison? Would you? If you would say something, what would it be? Why?

Read:

**Genesis 1:26-27
Judges 4:4-16
Galatians 3:23-28**

What would you do if you were Mr. Harrison?

What would you do if you were Allison?

What would you do if you were Sherri?

TAKE NOTES/MAKE NOTES

SHARING

Morgan was talking with her friend Elisa. Elisa knows everything about everybody and likes to "share". Morgan never tells Elisa anything she wouldn't also be willing to call up and tell the local popular radio station, because she knows it will get around just that fast.

According to Elisa, the guy that Morgan was dating last year, Mike, is going steady with Rene, "and they're, you know…doing it," Elisa says. Morgan brushes her off with an, "Oh well, hope they're happy."

Morgan remembers it was only a few weeks after she and Mike were going steady that he began to pressure her into things she didn't' want to do. He knew all the right things to say, and she did a lot of things she still regrets—but she wouldn't go all the way. He broke up with her soon after that.

Morgan never told anyone about what Mike ultimately wanted from her. It was just too personal. But Rene and Morgan used to sit at the same lunch table last year. Rene is so sweet.

DISCUSS:

@ **Is this just gossip? Should Morgan just ignore it? Why?**

@ **How do you think Morgan feels? Why?**

@ **What is Mike likely looking for in his relationship with Rene? What is Rene likely looking for in his relationship with Mike? Why?**

@ **What is the ultimate thing guys look for in a dating relationship? What is the ultimate thing girls are looking for? Is this true of all girls and all guys? Why?**

@ **Should Morgan say something to Rene? To Mike? What? Why?**

If a friend told you another friend was doing drugs, would you make an effort to find out the truth? Why? If a friend told you an enemy was doing drugs, would you make an effort to find out? Why? How does this apply to whether or not Morgan should say anything? Explain.

Proverbs 16:28
2 Thessalonians 3:11-13
1 Timothy 5:13

What would you do if you were Mike and your old girl-friend came and talked to you about this? Why?

What would you do if you were Rene?

What would you do if you were Morgan?

TAKE NOTES/MAKE NOTES

DREAMERS

Melanie loves and respects her father. He is a suit-and-tie business-man whose worked for the same company since before she was born. His life is well-ordered, predictable and properly prioritized.

As busy as he is, he never misses a recital. He's home every night by 6:00 p.m. for dinner. They always do great family activities on the weekend. Melanie listens to her friends complain and she thinks about how lucky she is.

A few weeks ago, she was cleaning the garage and found a box of her father's things from when he was in high school. She found essays and journals about traveling, stay-ing forever single, and the solemn vow to never settle down in one place.

To Melanie it appears that her father became everything he never wanted to be. She really wonders if her dad is truly happy. Is he going to freak out one day and just leave it all behind? Would she, like him (apparently), never realize the dreams she has in her heart right now?

DISCUSS:

@ Is there anything wrong with what Melanie's father has chosen for his life? Explain.

@ How much choice do you think Melanie's father had? How much choice do any of us have? Explain.

@ What were your parent's dreams when they were your age? How different are those dreams from their life? How are they the same? What can you learn from their "journey"?

@ Is it possible Melanie's dad is actually very happy—though his present life seems far different from his teenage dreams? Why? What's the best way for Melanie to find out?

@ Just as beauty is in the eyes of the beholder, how is happiness in the mind of the "live-er"? Explain.

Is it be fair to say that it was "God's plan" for Melanie's dad to be a businessman, even if he had something else in mind? Why?

How much of what we are is by our own choice and how much is by God's design? Explain.

 **Read:** 1 Corinthians 7:23
Philippians 3:12-14
Ecclesiastes 3:13

What would you do if you were Melanie?

TAKE NOTES/MAKE NOTES

SCREEN

Alfredo was home when the phone call came in at 8:30 a.m. asking him to show up for work at 10:00 a.m. instead of 3:00 p.m. He was screening the calls and didn't want to pick up. He also ignored the next three times his boss called that day.

When he showed up for work at 3:00 p.m., his boss was really mad and told him that he had been trying to get a hold of him after another employee called in sick. Apparently they lost customers that day because people were so frustrated waiting to be served that they just walked out. Alfredo said, "I never got the call."

@ **Did Alfredo lie? Technically, he never got the call. So, is that lying? Explain.**

@ **Make up a good definition for "lie." Explain.**

@ **Is it Alfredo's problem if someone else called in sick and service lagged? Why?**

@ **If someone is paying you what do you owe them?**

@ **Do you always have to do what your employer wants you to do or asks you to do? What if you don't feel like doing it or if it interferes with fun plans? Explain.**

@ **How would Jesus do your job the same as you? Differently than you? Why?**

**Psalm 35:20
Romans 7:11
Colossians 3:20**

@ **What would you do if you were Alfredo?**

GARRET'S HISTORY

There was absolutely no harm done when Garrett decided to blow off his history class and have lunch at the local burger place with his friends. The teacher was out for the day. His homework was done. He was holding onto a solid "A" in the class. The substitute was showing the same video that Garrett had seen in class last year.

There was nothing that could be gained by going, so what was the harm?

At dinner that evening, Garret's mother looked him right in the eye from across the table and said "So, how was your history class today?"

☞ Do you know when your parents "know"? How?

☞ Do you think Garrett's mother knows? Why?

☞ Would it be better at this point for Garrett to lie and take his chances, or confess? Why?

☞ What does "you play, you pay" mean? Explain.

☞ Do you typically end up paying when you "play," or do you just get to…play? Is it ultimately a good thing or a bad thing if you never have to pay when you "play"? Explain.

☞ Are there some things you should just do, even if you feel it's completely unnecessary? Like what? What happens if you disagree with a parent, teacher or church youth leader about what is necessary? If you disagree with a friend? Explain.

Romans 12:21
Hebrews 13:18
1 Corinthians 10-12

☞ What would you do if you were Garrett?

FAMILY

WHAT MOM DOESN'T KNOW

Abbey told her mother she was going to a concert with a bunch of friends. She didn't tell her mother that she would be driving herself there. She knew her mother thought she was riding in a group.

The concert is in a less-than-safe area of the city. Abbey's mother calls a few times during the concert and wants to know who Abbey will be riding home with and what route they intend to take home. Abbey manages to answer all the questions at least somewhat truthfully, but she knows she is not being completely forthcoming with all of the information.

Abbey just knows her mother will worry to the point of being hysterical and then throw a fit when she comes through the door. Her friends don't think Abbey's mom is hysterical and a worry wart, but Abbey sure does. She decides it's better to let her mother think what she wants to think.

TAKE NOTES/MAKE NOTES

DISCUSS:

@ What is a "lie of omission"? Is that what happened here? Did Abbey lie to her mother? Explain.

@ Should Abbey have done this? Why?

@ If her mother is hysterical, a perpetual worrier, a gloom-and-doom scenario-spouter, who has no trust in Abbey—does that make Abbey's choice right? What if her mother is reasonable, level-headed, and trusting—does that make Abbey's choice wrong? Why? Or does her mother have nothing to do with it—Abbey should just do the right thing? Why?

@ Have you ever let your parent "think what throwant to think" or is it better to try and communicate? Explain.

@ What could happen to Abbey? Do you think she thought this through well enough? Why?

@ Was Abbey's mom being over-protective? Explain.

@ What would you do if you were Abbey and you got back to your car to find the window broken out and the CD player gone?

@ How would you grade Abbey on her decision-making skills: A, B, C, D, or F? Why?

Read: Psalm 15:1-2
Isaiah 33:15-16
Proverbs 29:15

@ What would you do if you were Abbey?

TAKE NOTES/MAKE NOTES

NOTHING HAPPENED

Callie has been going out with Richard for several months. He's been trying to get her to have sex, which she always refuses. So far, she's had no problem telling him how far was too far, up until Friday.

That day, they were alone in his house and things went a little further than they ever had. They didn't have intercourse. In fact, she never took off her clothes. There was nothing more than some heated necking and some touching, but that was it.

Monday morning, Callie hears that Rich is telling all of his friends that Friday, they went all the way. The rumor spread through the school lightning fast, even a couple "concerned" teachers took her aside to ask her about what they were hearing.

The more Callie says nothing happened, the less people seem to believe her. What's going on?

DISCUSS:

@ **Why would a guy start a rumor like this? What's your opinion about him and what he did? Why?**

@ **Has anyone every started a rumor about you? Talk about it.**

@ **Have you ever spread such a rumor or done nothing to stop such a rumor from being spread? Why?**

@ **What's the harm of what Rich did? Can that harm be easily undone or made right? What's the message?**

@ **If the information people spread turns out to be true, does it count as gossip? Explain.**

@ **Why do you suppose we, as a society, are willing to believe the worst about others? Why are we so interested in negative information about others?**

@ **What's the difference between self-esteem and self-respect?**

 **Read:**

Psalm 42; Proverbs 11:3 Romans 12:19-21

◎ What would you do if you were Callie and your parents found out? If they didn't find out? Whether or not they found out?

◎ What would you do if you were Callie's best friend? Why?

◎ What would you do if you were Callie's father or mother—and you found out? Why?

TAKE NOTES/MAKE NOTES

THE PEOPLE IN YOUR NEIGHBORHOOD

Joyce's father has been asked to sign a petition to keep a low-income apartment building out of their neat, clean, solidly middle-class neighborhood. Joyce tells her father that everybody deserves a chance in life. Her father tells Joyce she has a lot to learn about the real world.

Joyce's father says he is not being prejudiced, but the fact of the matter is that the value of their house will go down if the apartment building goes up. As the safety level goes down, crime goes up. Gang activity goes up and property values go down.

Joyce's father has all the research in front of him. It looks like what he says has been proven true in other neighborhoods.

TAKE NOTES/MAKE NOTES

DISCUSS:

◎ Why is Joyce so adamant about her position? Why is her father so adamant?

◎ Is it true that you are "part of the problem or part of the solution"? Explain.

◎ Tell of a time when you stood up for what's right even though it was going to hurt you or cost you. Why did you do it?

◎ Do you ever argue with someone who has "all the facts" in front of them? Why?

◎ How do you argue for the existence of God with no tangible proof?

◎ Does everyone have "a little" prejudice in them? Explain.

Read:

Joshua 23:11-13
Mathew 9:11
Luke 6:20-36
Acts 17:24-26

◎ What would you do if you were Joyce?

TAKE NOTES/MAKE NOTES

UNCERTAIN TERMS

Carter was not going to win any physical fitness awards anytime soon. He sort of enjoyed his "computer-geek" reputation. He was small, wore glasses and could still fit in the clothes he wore in 8th grade. He was a junior now.

Yesterday, Carter saw two guys from his required gym glass break the window on the principal's car. They know he saw them. This morning the two guys cornered him and told him in no uncertain terms, that if he opened his mouth, they would be happy to break it for him.

NOTE: After a little debate about Carter's options, read the study again with the this ending:

Carter saw a guy from his gym class arguing with his girlfriend. The girl was upset and the guy was getting angry. Finally, the guy punched the locker right next to the girl's head. She began to cry and ran off. The guy saw Carter and told him in no uncertain terms that if he opened his mouth, the guy would be happy to break it for him.

TAKE NOTES/MAKE NOTES

DISCUSS:

@ What are Carter's options? Explain.

@ What is the right thing to do in both cases?

@ Would you do the right thing if you were in his place? Why?

@ If Carter was directly confronted by the principal about the incident, what then? Why?

@ Why do you think telling adults or authorities about problems, crimes, or bad things they've witnessed earns people names like, "tattle-tale," "whistle blower," "squealer," "fink," "rat"? Why such a negative connotation?

@ Is there ever a time to break the "code of silence," and tell an adult or the authorities about something you've seen? Why? If your friend has been down for a long time and threatens to kill himself, but makes you promise you will tell no one—should you tell someone? Why?

@ What happens when you keep information to yourself about illegal activity or someone's plan to harm himself or someone else?

@ Do you think teachers and other authority figures rely too much on tattle-tales? Is that justified? Why? Run the guys in? Why?

Read:

Romans 12:17-19
James 1:19

@ Would Carter be justified in turning the guys in?

@ Should he talk to the guys? Why or why not?

TAKE NOTES/MAKE NOTES

FUN AND GAMES

Tina is eighteen and lost her virginity on her 17th birthday. She has been with several guys over the last year. She doesn't think of herself as a slut or anything like that. She likes "doing stuff" with her boyfriends. And she almost never went all the way unless she really felt she liked the guy or if she was the one who wanted it. To her a little "fun and games" in the backseat is no big deal.

Tina's mother knows that her daughter is going off to college soon so she asked Tina to sit down so they could have "the talk". Tina can't believe how out dated her mother's thinking is. Her mother wants Tina to ask lots of questions; Tina already believes she knows the answers so she has none.

The conversation grows more and more uncomfortable as Tina mother slowly begins to realize that the talk may be too little to late.

DISCUSS:

❷ Does Tina have much else to learn about sex or is she pretty much a sex expert because she has had sex with a number of guys? Why?

❷ Have you ever had "the talk" with one of your parents? How'd it go?

❷ Is there anything you would not tell your mother? Why?

❷ Do you think your parents know as much about sex as their sexually active kids do?

❷ If you stonewall your parents in duscussing sex, do you have a right to go to them if you get in trouble?

❷ Can you picture Tina's mom's point of view?

 **Read:** Romans 12:1-21
1 Corinthians 6:19
Proverbs 5:7-14

◉ What would you do if you were Tina's mother?

◉ What would you do if you were Tina?

◉ What would you say if you were Tina's youth minister if you became aware Tina was sexually active?

TAKE NOTES/MAKE NOTES

IT'S AN ART

Dana is taking his fourth year of high school art. It is his senior year and he is serious enough about what he does to think about being an artist as a career. He likes the teacher and has thought about being an art teacher.

There are only four other students in art class at this level and three of them are there because they thought it would be a free ride. The teacher allows the group to work at his or her own pace and Dana is quite a bit ahead of the others.

Twice now, someone has purposely damaged Dana's work when no one else should be in the room. He has mentioned this to his teacher, but the teacher says, "I wasn't in the room."

Dana has had to start over and notices how suspiciously quiet some of the others are, when he discovers that his own work has been destroyed. At the end of the school day today, Dana realizes he left his history book in the art room. He runs to the room so he can still catch the bus.

The door is unlocked. The teacher is gone. Dana knows the artwork of the students he thinks damaged his stuff. The setting is perfect for a little payback.

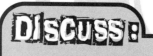

🌀 Is there any truth to the old adage "Revenge is a dish that is best served cold"? Why? What does this mean?

🌀 What if Dana had proof of who damaged his projects? Should that make a difference in his decision? Why?

🌀 What if Dana ruined their artwork and then found out he was wrong?

🌀 What if the others report Dana to the teacher?

🌀 What would happen if Dana got caught? Why?

Romans 12:17-19
Matthew 6:14-15
Ephesians 4:26
James 1:19

🌀 What would you do if you were Dana?

TWIST

Jonathan is an assistant manager at the Twisty Treats Ice Cream Shop. His boss has offered to let him sit in on several job interviews to learn about hiring and because he values Jonathan's opinion.

There is one position open for weekend work and Jonathan recognizes one of the applicants as a kid from school. He is an atheist who loves to argue with others about the existence of God. That aside, this kid does the best in his interview. On that basis, he deserves the job.

Jonathan knows religious preference isn't supposed to be considered when hiring a person. He just doesn't want to spend his working hours endlessly debating someone on matters of faith. Jonathan is weighing whether or not to bring this matter up with his boss—without sounding prejudiced.

DISCUSS:

- Should "atheist" be considered a religious preference? Why?

  - If Jonathan says, "don't hire him," is that Christian? Why?

- Should Jonathan have a choice in who he works with? Why?

  - Who was the most difficult person you've ever worked with (at school, at work, or at church)?

- Have you have been discriminated against because of your beliefs? Talk about it.

  - Should religion be talked about in the workplace? Why?

- What would happen if Jonathan handed out the ice cream to customers and said "God loves you"—would that be imposing his Christian beliefs on others? Why?

Read:

Galatians 3:26-28
1 John 3:15
Acts 10:34-35

- What would you do if you were Jonathan?

DESTRUCTION

Phil needed more cash. He arged with his parents about whether or not taking on a part-time job was too much for his schedule. He finally persuaded them by assuring them that he would set aside a portion of every check for his college savings account and give to the church. He would have "a little extra cash" when he needed it.

So far, he had been great about managing his money. Today he saw the new, *Destruction Derby 3* video game at the mall. Phil loved the first two *Destruction Derby* games and can barely wait to buy the new one.

If he waits and saves up his money, it will take a month. The idea comes to him that if he withholds his college and church money from his current paycheck, he could buy the game today! All he'd have to do is take a little more out of his next few paychecks for college savings and church giving.

@ Make up a working definition of "maturity." Does Phillip fit into it? Why?

@ Who makes your financial decisions? Buys your clothes? Do you save for college or other things? How much do you have in the bank? Do you know?

@ Do you know anyone who makes a lot of promises but never seems to come through? What do you think about that? Why?

@ What are some good reasons for Phil to keep his promise and wait to buy the game? Which is the best reason?

@ Would it be that big a deal to break his promise to his parents? Does, "what they don't know can't hurt them" apply? Why?

 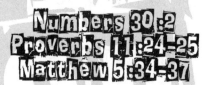

Numbers 30:2
Proverbs 11:24-25
Matthew 5:34-37

@ What would you do if you were Phillip's parents?

@ What would you do if you were Phillip?

LIKE A MAN

Jamal and several of his friends are hanging out at the mall on Saturday afternoon, before a movie. They are sitting in the food court, watching pretty girls.

A man and his son are sitting nearby. The young boy spills his drink while playing with his free prize from his kid's meal. The father promptly takes the toy and tosses it into the garbage.

The boy begins to cry and the father threatens to backhand him. The kid sits sniffling for a moment and the dad says, "Oh, grow up. Act like a man!"

DISCUSS:

@ How would you react to such a scene? How do you feel about the dad? Why?

@ Would you say anything? What if, instead of taking a toy from a child, the man was hitting his wife? Is that different? Why?

@ Have you ever seen a parent hit his or her child in public? What was the situation? How did you react? Is it ever okay for a parent to strike their child? To do so in public? Why?

@ Have you ever been hit in public? Talk about it.

@ Do we have the right to judge how others raise their children? How they discipline their children? Why?

@ Why do you think some abused people (adults or children) continue to stay in the home with their abuser?

Read: Matthew 19:13-15
Ephesians 6:4
Colossians 3:21

@ Are some things unforgivable? Why?

AND THEY'LL KNOW WE ARE CHRISTIANS

Only Christian guys!" That's what Ellen hears when she asks her mother about dating. Ellen has dated both Christian and non-Christian guys. It has been her experience that Christians are worse than non-Christians to date.

Her mother doesn't want to hear this. Her mother asked the opinion of several parents in her Bible Study group and they all agreed that Christians should only date other Christians. She even has scripture to back it up.

Ellen is angry to hear that her mother made her dating decision the "topic of the week" for the Bible study group. Ellen feels those folks have enough to talk about without getting into her life. For example, she knows that one of the parents in her mother's group has no idea how physical her son tries to get on dates—Ellen wouldn't go out with him in a million years.

Ellen has been asked out by a really great guy, on the honor roll, part-time job, respectful to his elders, and a volunteer at a shelter...he's also Jewish.

TAKE NOTES/MAKE NOTES

DISCUSS:

◉ What kinds of problems might you encounter if you date or marry someone outside your faith? Can love alone overcome all those problems? Explain.

◉ There was a time when interracial marriages were illegal. As far as you are concerned, should they still be? How about dating? Why?

◉ Do you think Ellen's parents would have a problem if she intended to marry someone of another race, as long as he was Christian? Why?

◉ Are you a racist if you don't want your children to date or marry someone of another race? Explain.

◉ Have you ever experienced prejudice because of your beliefs? Because of your race? What was that like?

◉ How important is religion to you when you are deciding whether or not to date someone? Is every date a possible mate? Is religion not an important matter unless you plan to marry someone of another faith? Why?

Read: **Amos 3:3; James 2:5-7 Colossians 3:11 Ephesians 6:13**

◉ What would you do if you were Ellen?

◉ What would you do if you were Ellen's mother?

TAKE NOTES/MAKE NOTES

WITNESS

Mike, Pat and Tony all went to the same youth group and had known each other since they were little kids. Pat had a friend named Bill that he invited to church several times. The four boys got along well in school and sat at the same lunch table, but Bill always seemed uncomfortable in the church.

At a Wednesday night Bible study on witnessing/ sharing faith, the entire senior high group decided that they would all wear Christian T-shirts to school on Fridays. They wouldn't try and push anything on anyone, but it anyone asked, they would be glad to share.

Pat told Bill about what the youth group was doing and asked him if he wanted to borrow a Christian shirt and join them. Bill said he already had one.

On Friday morning, the kids from the youth group were all wearing various T-shirts with Christian symbols and slogans. Bill came in a T-shirt he made himself, featuring Jesus in a "Groucho" mask.

Q Are religious T-shirts allowed at your school? What is the policy? Would you wear one? Why?

Q Is it worse to be too pushy in sharing your faith or not being pushy enough? Why? If we were to err, which side do you think God would have us err on—too pushy or not pushy? Explain.

Q Is it sacrilegious to show Santa at the manger? How about the Easter Bunny at the empty tomb?

Q How will people likely react to Bill's shirt? Why? Do you think Jesus would laugh at Bill's shirt? Explain.

Q Would it be okay if it were a principal or the President on the T-shirt? Why?

Q Why are some people so uptight about the way that Jesus is depicted? Since no one is sure what Jesus looked like, can't we make him look like just about anything and be okay? Why?

Read:

**Philippians 3:7-10;
Proverbs 20:11
Job 8:21**

◉ What would you do if you were Mike, Pat, or Tony?

TAKE NOTES/MAKE NOTES

AMMUNITION

Pete and his younger brother Marty have shared a room since Marty was old enough to be out of a crib. Marty is six years younger than Pete. Pete is now 17 and his little brother is driving him crazy.

They've always had a rule about staying out of each other's stuff. This has never been a problem for Pete, since he has no desire to get into his brother's stuff. But Marty is almost constantly rummaging through, or using Pete's stuff.

Pete came home from school and found one of his best CD's broken on the floor. He also found one of his video games sitting in a puddle of soda pop, on top of the game system. He got mad and started yelling at his little brother. Pete told Marty that he was going to tell their parents.

Marty said if he told them about the ruined CD and video game, that he would tell them that Pete had been alone in the house with a girl last week (something Marty was not allowed to do). Marty had walked in on Pete and the girl in the living room.

TAKE NOTES/MAKE NOTES

DISCUSS:

How would you stop an escalating argument like this one if you were in it? If you were tired of listening to it? Why?

What kind of secrets should you absolutely never share—even for your annoying younger brother or aggravating older brother? Why?

How important is it for your friends or brothers and sisters to be able to keep your secrets? Why?

Are you keeping a secret for anyone right now? Why?

Is anyone keeping your secrets? Explain. Who are the people you absolutely trust to keep your secrets? Explain.

Has anyone ever threatened to reveal your secrets? Did they? What happened?

What are some other things that younger brothers and sisters pull on older siblings? What are some ways older brothers and sisters aggravate younger brothers and sisters?

Read: Proverbs 25:8-10
Proverbs 17:12-14

What would you do if you were Pete and Marty's parent and overheard everything?

What would you do if you were Pete?

What would you do if you were Marty?

TAKE NOTES/MAKE NOTES

FRIENDS

ACCEPTANCE, DISHONESTY, FRIENDSHIP

COMING ATTRACTIONS

Candice and some of her new friends decided they would all go to the movies together on Saturday afternoon. There would be six of them in all.

One of the girls called Candice and asked her to call Robin and ask her not to come. Robin was a Christian and even though she didn't talk about it much, as a result, a couple girls felt Robin thought she had a stuck-up, superior attitude. They also didn't want her giving them a hard time on their movie choice.

Candice doesn't want to get her new friends mad at her, so she agreed to call. She reached Robin's voice mail and left a message, "We're not going to the movies on Saturday after all. I'll talk to you on Monday."

The girls have a great time at the movies, until the lights came up and all five saw Robin sitting directly behind them.

"Good movie, huh?" Robin said.

@ **What is your definition of a friend?**

@ **What is the most important quality of a friend? Explain.**

@ **Why is being accepted so important that, to gain it, sometimes we will hurt each other?**

@ **Tell of a time when you were hurt or betrayed by a friend who was pursuing the acceptance of others.**

@ **What is the most you've ever forgiven a friend? Talk about it.**

@ **What is the most you've ever been forgiven? Talk about it.**

2 Kings 2:2
John 15:13
Proverbs 18:24
Ephesians 4:25

@ **What would you do if you were Robin?**

@ **What would you do if you were Candice?**

HONOR

Pierce's favorite band is the Slut Puppies. He has all three of their CD's. His parents, on the other hand, are not Slut Puppies fans at all. In fact, Pierce made an agreement with his parents that, if they are in the house, he would only listen to the Slut Puppies on headphones.

When Pierce found out the Slut Puppies were going to be in town, he asked his mother's permission to go. She said he could go as long as he brought his math grade up, did extra credit in both English and History and used his own money to buy the ticket.

When the time came for the tickets to go on sale, his father said that he had a friend at work who told him some of the lyrics in the Slut Puppies songs. He'd also heard a teenage girl had overdosed at a Slut Puppies concert last year.

His father is adamant, "I don't care what your mother said. I'm telling you, you can't go."

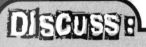

● **When have you been caught between your parents in one of their disagreements? Because they have not communicated clearly with one another? How did it work out?**

● **Is Pierce's dad being unfair or just doing his job as a dad? Explain.**

● **From what you've heard from your parents, did they have music that alarmed your grandparents? How did they handle it?**

● **How are your standards for selecting music different from your parent's standards? How are they the same? Ultimately, are your parent's standards fair and reasonable? Explain.**

● **Overall, what are the rules for music you can and can't listen to in your home?**

● **How do you talk to your parents when you think they are being unreasonable? What could you improve about the way you challenge them when you disagree?**

Romans 12:18; Leviticus 4:5 Ephesians 6:1-4; James 4:17

● **What would you do if you were Pierce's mother? Father?**

● **What would you do if you were Pierce?**

● **Is there a compromise here? What is it?**

PAYING THE PRICE

Sean's parents got divorced last year. Sean was really hurt. His grades went in the toilet. His attitude was horrible. He got involved in some vandalism and picked a bunch of fights—he was so angry all the time.

Now he's been resurrected from his "valley of death," as he calls it, and is back on his game. In fact, it seems as though Sean has never been happier.

Sean has been dating a girl who goes to a conservative church. One day, in tears, she tells him that his parents are destined for Hell because they were divorced. Because of what they've done, the whole family is living against God's law and the whole family will pay the price.

Sean can't believe it. Since the divorce, his parents have never been happier and he's never felt better. Divorce was a really good thing for his family.

TAKE NOTES/MAKE NOTES

DISCUSS:

@ Is divorce the unpardonable sin? How does God view divorce?

@ How should people view divorce? Explain.

@ What do you think of the idea that God will punish a family because the parents divorce? Explain.

@ Does divorce contribute to juvenile delinquency? Explain.

@ Can anybody live by all of the "rules" in the book? What are the most important ones? Why?

@ In regard to Heaven, who has the right to say who is and who isn't "getting in?" Why?

@ Why do you think some people use the Christian faith as a sort of license to judge others? Is that supposed to be job #1 for Christians, or is something else supposed to be? Explain.

Read:

Matthew 5:31-32
Ephesians 5:21-33

@ What would you do if you were Sean?

TAKE NOTES/MAKE NOTES

DIVORCE, SIN, FORGIVENESS